on the page

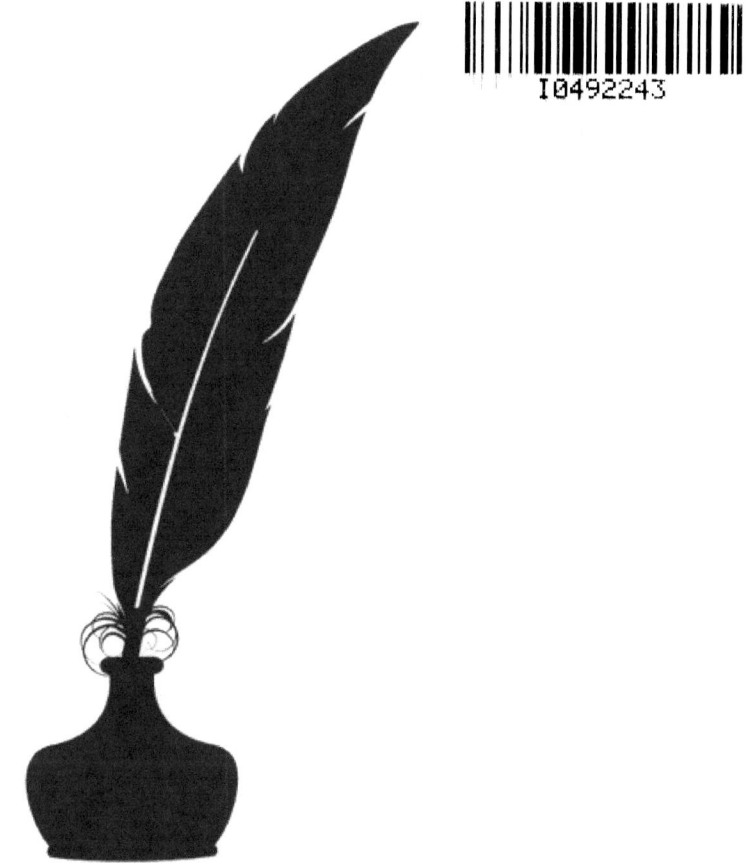

poems for artists, writers, and other hooligans

Kevin Trent Boswell

ISBN: 9798690104429

on the page

CONTENTS

DEDICATION i

Introduction iii

Acknowledgements xi

the poetry fairies 1

preaching pleasures 2

Poets Have It Easy 4

At First Glance 11

no poet is without honor, save on his own planet 12

plan 13

That Says It All 14

poets 16

Misquoted 17

new poem. 18

magnetism 19

small words 20

Improv 21

ah, creation!! 22

Ooops. 24

sugar 27

Visa 28

Still On Pause 30

A Thought Not Worth Writing Down 31

if you want to be a poet 32

Suicide 36

untitled 37

Stake Out 38

untitled 39

drop 40

What's On? 42

Koan 43

it's just poetry 44

you wouldn't know	46
a pinch of madness	50
untitled	52
untitled	53
We Miss Things	54
shine	57
victories	58
afterward	60
The Bricks of Lonely Night	61
blank slate	74
Poetry Sundays	76
A Thousand and One	80
haiku charades	81
almost something like it	82
a thousand pardons	83
canned biscuits	84
stain	86
emblem	91
circa 1929	92
rain	96
scorpion, fish, eagle	100
Mind Game	101
restaurants and rough days	102
;	105
untitled	106
morning	107
butcher, baker, poetry maker	108
Birthday For John Michael	112
Car Trouble	118
Rose Garden	119
Clipping Smilax	120
untitled	125
long play	126

jack-in-the-box   130

persistence   136

fabulous   138

it's a bit forced, isn't it?   139

pocket change   140

untitled   141

rain on paper   142

Once   145

untitled   146

untitled   148

prodigy   149

untitled   152

wind up toy   154

small   155

Clarity   156

To Jazz   157

pick me up something sweet   158

Preacher   160

minimum wage   162

I need   163

untitled   164

it's a lovely piece, miss   168

Beef Jerky   171

reverie   172

Aptitude Testing   174

untitled   177

untitled   178

sad haiku   180

seasoned grease blues   181

two choruses, no more   182

great things   184

After Taxes   186

punch clock   187

On The Way Back	188
untitled	189
this book	190
untitled	194
Ben's Word	197
untitled	203
Ghost Writer	206
Part-Time	207
So, you really liked it?	209
untitled	210
Underwater	211
haiku zero	212
hindsight	213
ABOUT THE AUTHOR	214

DEDICATION

This book is for any artist who sincerely strives to produce the most authentic realization of their craft. These poems are for you who create, regardless of your medium. I dedicate it to you who candidly go for the throat of your vision, never settling for half-measures.

The amount of mental, emotional, and even spiritual stress on a truthful artist can never be overstated. The frequent and often total failure of the public to *grok* what art means or represents, the endless stream of criticism, the lack of exposure, compensation, appreciation, and recognition are truly soul-sucking. Attempting to move against the grain of complaints from family, friends, fans, publishers, agents, and the public, in general, is no small task.

For this reason, I am ever a fan of the underdog artist who crafts their unique purpose and vision, especially when facing seemingly unbearable pressures to move in a different direction. I stand beside all of you who manifest what you see, hear and feel deep inside instead of what is merely popular or profitable.

I consecrate this book in the names of all true artists. This book is for you who move with courage toward your Muse. Note that I said *courage* and not *fearlessness*. Where there is no fear, there is no great overcoming of fear. Great victory stems from great challenge. I ask you to stand firm. Let your light shine forth. Share your truest vision of the universe, the world, and *yourself*. Wealth and fame be damned. Do not allow yourself to become beholden to approval. Follow your vision and your muse.

For they who slit their own throats
Spilling blood upon the altar of art
For them who glue the words together
After the thing itself has fallen apart

To you who dip your quills into the bitter
As well as into the sweet and good
May this sustain you as you capture
All of those ideas that no one else could

Introduction

on the page is a collection of poems. That much is straightforward. In one sense, it's a bunch of poems about poetry itself, about being a poet, knowing other poets, and all the myriad experiences that poets and writers in general have.

It's about wrestling with creativity and the difficulties of separating imagination from neurosis or eccentricity. It's the lament of rejections from publishers and zines and poetry journals, the uncomfortable silence that we sometimes feel after reading a piece at an open mic, how that creates doubt and stings the ego. It's the joy of having one or perhaps a roomful of people who love your work and trying to recreate that experience.

It's about the isolation of being an artisan of a craft rarely practiced anymore. It's about feeling those ostracizing pangs when you see mindless masses eating up and doting on someone's work, when you, as well as all the other writers you know, agree that it's garbage. It's about hacking through the jungle of the day job, wanting only to go home and write. It's about having plenty of time and finding that the words will not come. In short, this is art for artists. But that's not all that it is.

on the page isn't just a bunch of pieces about poetry and poets and "poeting." There are quite a few works in this volume that are *not* about writing and being a writer. I chose these pieces because, regardless of their merit, *something clicked for me while writing them*. These poems and bits of prose are pieces that helped me somehow *actually feel like a writer*.

Some might find that statement surprising since they may think that *all* of them would produce such a feeling, or at least *most*. But if you've logged very many hours of trying to be a writer yourself, then you know that it's a feeling one does not simply *switch on*. At times it can be somewhat elusive and difficult to conjure up. Sometimes you page this tenuous emotion but the feeling that answers the call is one of doubt and insecurity. *You're not good enough. Oh, that's cute*; you *think you're a real writer. Don't quit your day job* and other types of mental self-sabotage.

Writers don't exist in a vacuum. Writers are somebody's sons, daughters, wives, husbands, and employees. You take in the opinions of those around you, whether or not you want to. They affect you and tuning out the particularly nasty, unhelpful ones can be a gigantic task. Some people try to help, and others try to take you down a notch or two. Even when you recognize what they're doing when they say, "Don't quit your day job," it still hurts, and you still have to process that.

Now, I'd be among the first to tell you that, even if you're an *incredible* author, poet, playwright, etc., *you probably shouldn't quit your day job*. That's because it's pretty challenging to make any money through writing and especially challenging with poetry. But I'd encourage you to *keep writing* and *keep trying*.

To be a full-time artist of any sort, you'd have to know that you were steadily making enough money to cover all your living expenses, and for most writers, the profits they earn on their writing are little more than a bit of extra spending cash. Writers, like most dancers, actors, musicians, sculptors, photographers, and other artisans, do not create their art for money; they make it because *they have to*. It's a spiritual calling, even among atheists, *especially* among atheists. Some of the pieces in this book wrestle with all that *spiritual hubbub*, as well.

Hearing poetry is often *a transcendent experience* —your poetry can be if you're lucky— and that's as it should be. Art is a balm for the soul. Art heals the soul of the creator, as well as anyone who views it or hears it, as long as *they choose to open up to it*. This brings us to a modern challenge: that of the times in which we live.

As strenuous as things were in, say, the sixties, I believe that we live in a much more difficult time. The population has exploded since then, it's hotter (due to climate change), and resources are more fiercely fought over than ever. Since the baby boomer generation, we've spawned vast numbers of entirely self-indulgent, lazy, stupid, and highly narcissistic antisocial parasites. If it's not their own Instagram feed or hearing you tell them how hot they look, they're not interested.

Such wastes of space are not opening themselves up to your art. They're not listening to what you say, even when you're warning them to get out of the way of a speeding truck; they're certainly not going to read your novel, poetry book, or short story. Even if they did sit through your documentary that you spent months and tons of money on, they wouldn't understand it.

I think that, while such twits have been around since the dawn of civilization, they're proliferating, the idiot ranks growing exponentially. This creates a drought of good art and good artists, but that's a much smaller part of the overall equation.

The bigger problem is that there's not much audience for good art anymore because the *average* person is just too damn stupid to read a comic strip, much less a play. Before anyone gets insulted, if you've read this far, be of good cheer; you are NOT one of the morons I'm referring to. Their eyes would have rolled back into their skulls after four or five sentences, tops.

We have many brilliant people who would love to read more, watch more good movies, and hit the art shows. They just can't. They're too busy trying to make ends meet. They're stressed out to the max. Even if they buy your book, fully intending to read it, they will likely get hit by some new onslaught of problems that causes them to feel too much stress to pick it up.

If they do pick it up and read it, they don't enjoy it because they're so worried about bill collectors, the possibility of losing their job, their kids, etc., that they just read the same four sentences over and over. They are in a PTSD trance that doesn't allow the medicine to work. And your art (if it's good) is indeed *medicine*, a *desperately needed* medicine.

> It is difficult to get the news from poems
> yet men die miserably every day
> for lack of what is found there.
>
> —William Carlos Williams, poet

When I said that certain pieces helped me feel like a "real poet," I did not mean that I had any feeling of greatness, either about the works or about myself. The writing of these particular poems made me feel *as if I was doing what I was supposed to be doing at the time.* I felt as if I was born to write those particular poems.

Some are simple, uncomplicated pieces, poems that don't necessarily stand out as being among the best in my repertoire. With others, I did feel as if I was on the cusp of something great. Now, I may be the only one to ever feel that way about them, but this matters very little. That feeling may have been only during the initial inspiration or after completing the piece. In some cases, I had the feeling the whole way through. Regardless, these pieces felt like they came from *a real writer*. Far more important, this is art that I felt I was supposed to *share with other artists*.

Whether you enjoy them or not is none of my business. My business was to write them and share them. *I've done that now*. Perhaps the book will hit you powerfully, start to finish. Maybe you'll think a few of the poems are good, and the rest are garbage, perhaps the other way around. But you can't lose on this. You might have in your hands a new gem for your library, something to discuss with your friends, especially if they're also artists. If not, you'll at least have some paper for a cold winter night when you need to get the fireplace going. It will serve you well in at least one of these scenarios.

I didn't want to reuse too many previously published pieces, so please understand that my other books have many such works in them as well, pieces that would be good to share with other artists. But I've only chosen a scant two or three pieces to use in this book that were already in print.

One example is *aptitude testing*. This was first published in the book *Next* because it fits well there. Honestly, it sits even better in this collection than in *Next*. An example of a piece that could have been included here (but is not) is the poem *empty rooms*, from my book *Chaos Comes Apart*. I might have easily repurposed it for this book. I wrote that piece when I was still very young; I couldn't have been more than twenty years old. I believe that piece was in my very first poetry notebook, somewhere between age sixteen and eighteen. And yet, I may never again write anything as solid as that poem.

As simple, sparse, and unassuming as that poem is, I'm exceedingly proud of it. It leaves tons of space for personal interpretation, for the reader to apply it to their own life. Yet, most people who comment on it tell me of the haunting, lonely feeling it evokes. In short, *empty rooms* is everything that I believe poetry is supposed to be.

Again, that feeling may reside solely within my being, which is perfectly OK. I want to encourage other writers to embrace this stance with their work, to strive less to find that voice that sells lots of books, paintings, etc., and work to create something that *impresses the hell out of you*. When you happen to hear that voice coming from you, don't suppress it, that's *your genius*. Your genius work might not put bread on the table, but you can always create *other things* that will. Besides, you probably have a day job for paying bills. When you find yourself down or even seemingly out, you won't particularly care if you produced something at some point that was very popular or profitable if you didn't believe in it.

If you saw a beautiful painting and no one else ever saw it, that work still existed *for you*, and it was no less attractive. In the same way, you might produce art that most people are never aware of, but a handful of people will be radically moved by, perhaps even *forever changed*.

Years ago, I saw a mural at a hotel in Wrightsville Beach, NC. The mural was whales and dolphins near the swimming pool. I never met that artist, and the mural didn't particularly move me. I doubt seriously if even he felt it was his best work; it was probably only done to pay the bills.

But there was an interesting, six degrees of separation type connection between him and me. His name was Sam Ray, and we both dated the same woman. I'd never met him because (unfortunately) he killed himself before I even knew the girl we mutually knew.

Sam also wrote poetry, and this girl shared some of it with me. He wrote a beautiful piece called *Sam Ray's Handbook of Really Important Stuff*. I don't know if I correctly recall the title, and I don't remember most of it, but one part stuck with me. This work was a sort of dictionary, with fairly long and amusing entries about a wide variety of things, ideas, places, people, etc. It was all insightful, moving, and clever. But what struck me most and stuck with me, all these many years later, was one particularly brief entry:

> **Women:** Women are soft, angelic creatures who speak in tongues.
>
> —Sam Ray, Sam Ray's Handbook of Really Important Stuff

I don't think Sam's *Handbook* was ever published, but at least one entry certainly made its mark on me, and now, *I have passed it on to you*. This is precisely how art lives on inside of us. When you create art, you may affect generations of people you will never meet.

Jim Morrison reportedly said that if we had a nuclear war, if almost everything was destroyed, yet there were survivors, the only thing that would live on would be scraps of poetry and music, things that people already had in their memory.

Perhaps bits of this book will hit you and stick with you. Maybe none of it will; it doesn't matter. What matters is that *I'm doing the work I am supposed to do*. I hope you find (and do) what you were born to do. May this inspire you to push forward and do what you are here to do.

> Can anything be sadder than work left unfinished?
>
> Yes, work never begun.
>
> —Christina Rossetti, poet

Acknowledgements

This book is partly for every teacher I ever had who taught literature, art, music, history, poetry, etc., and did so with intelligence and enthusiasm. You all had an impact on me, and I thank you.

But I want to give a special thanks to my dear friend Jim Owens. When I was only eighteen years old, I loaned him a notebook of my poetry. This was unsettling enough for the apparent risk of exposing one's art to another human being because Jim was my guitar mentor. Jim was the lead guitarist in my very first band, The Intruders. We were a southern rock and blues cover band with a few originals, and I need to tell the story for context.

I'd landed the position as rhythm guitarist entirely by accident. It belonged to my former guitar teacher. My teacher invited me to come to his band's practice session to inspire me and show me what a real, working band looks like. I showed up, but he did not.
So there I was, with three guys I'd never met. Jim was the lead guitarist, and they asked me if I wanted to sit in. I nervously said yes. They said I played well and had a good grasp of some songs they were doing. They said, "Come back next week," and I did.

Again, I showed up while my teacher did not. They said he was fired and asked me if I wanted to be the rhythm guitarist. The prospect of filling my teacher's shoes with a bunch of guys that I'd just met was a weighty idea for an unsure eighteen-year-old. I felt guilty; it was as if I'd stolen my teacher's band.

In reality, he'd gotten himself fired whether or not I replaced him. They assured me they would have reverted to a three-piece band anyway; I was just a lucky accident. So, I felt much better until they said, "We have forty songs. The first gig is in two weeks. Be ready." That was sarcasm; I was terrified.

I only knew about a fourth of them. *Panic.* I was the lowly, unproven, and very young *backup* guitarist, in a band of guys twice my age, each with lots of gigging experience. Jim was an excellent guitarist. He'd played professionally since he was sixteen. I'd watch him play the blistering lead parts of Allman Brothers songs and ZZ Top, Lynyrd Skynyrd, and Eric Clapton tunes. He'd even opened for Skynyrd and other big-name bands; Jim was a hero to me.

Of course, there was a little of the expected (even needed) goodnatured hazing that bandmates give each other; boys will be boys, after all. Outside of this, Jim was *courteous* to me; far more courteous than a grown man needed to be with an eighteen-year-old kid. He was much more helpful than most guitarists would have been. Most would have let their egos get in the way. He did not.

Jim had me come to his house every day of those two weeks, and he tutored me in detail on all the material that I needed for the gig. We'd pour over however many songs we could, getting everything *just so.* He'd teach me until my brain was full for the day and I couldn't grasp anything else.

He'd give me a couple of bong hits of his homegrown weed, strong enough to incapacitate a horse, *an ornery horse.* Once I recovered (no small task), I'd go to work, then home to sleep, get up and start practicing until it was time to go back to his house again.

He wasn't arrogant; he was patient and encouraging. Now, Jim is a proud man, not exactly known for being the most diplomatic guy in the room. Insult him, and he's as likely to pop you in the mouth as he is to tell you nine ways that you can go fuck yourself. Still, we became friends quickly. At first, it was just business, but once he realized I wouldn't turn into a self-absorbed asshole after I became "one of the guys," he accepted me into his circle. He treated me as family.

The subject of poetry came up, and I learned that Jim was a big fan of Emily Dickinson, so he knew good work when he saw it. I loaned him a notebook of my poetry. I only asked him to read a few pieces and share any thoughts he had. To my surprise, he read the whole thing. Not only had he read them, but he gave insightful feedback. He *understood* them. That was something that I'd not encountered before.

He said to his wife, with total sincerity, "Kevin is *a true poet*." That simple affirmation, while it was only one man's opinion, it was enough to encourage me to keep writing and striving. It was more than enough.

> One may never truly know
> Into what deep and secret part
> A simple kindness, how it grows
> Seed taking root in the heart
>
> The depth of its vast potential
> That seeming, but not, small event
> How vital, immense and essential
> When it sprouts, or where it went

—from *in the current*

the poetry fairies

mischievous siblings of creation
dance around my head
mocking me
whispering into my ear
though they know well
I heard not what they said

I'm stuck for
words and phrases
that sing
but still, they prance,
mimic, and sting

                you'll know us not,
                though we know you!

                we give you only
                what we wish to!

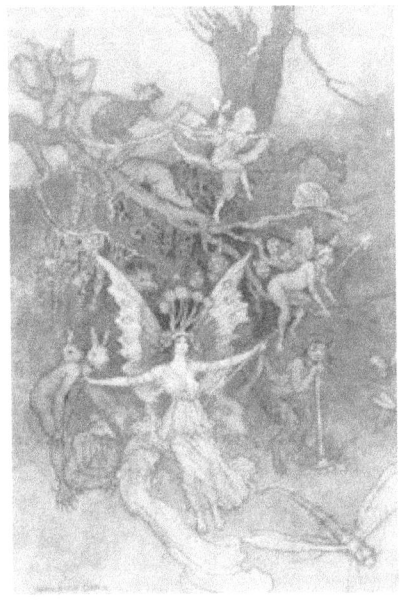

preaching pleasures

a marvelous theology
clever structure
shiny words

language,
art of husbandry
the pleasuring of herds

diagrams and pictures
quilting timeline,
complete

adherence
frigid tradition
cannot compete

dance the weak edges
of frontal cortex
inspire

they learn
each, every time
to forget you're a liar

trouble not details
fill dull gaps
with gloss

it's easier
to swallow shiny
than to chew on the dross

mob hanging mad dog
brewing coup boils
a reckoning

gathering cloud
masses, now black
gallows smile beckoning

today's bending is all
over backward,
it thanks you

waking
beast of remorse
public, it spanks you

Poets Have It Easy

What more could one ask for?

Simply take a basic framework,
one that has been previously formulated
installed, worked free of most glitches,
bugs, hang-ups, discrepancies, etc

Then you merely reshape it to convey a mood
tone, feelings, emotions, circumstances
(extenuating or otherwise)
details of the environment
in which they took place and form;
even if they never took place
anywhere except in one's head

You might say they have it made

> *That's the way you do it*
> *money for nothin'*
> *and your chicks for free*

No struggle
no discomfort or displacement

Nope
just living a wild life of romance and adventure

Being paid
PAID, mind you...
for expressing yourself
giving your opinions to the general public

Everyone loves you and respects you
you get invited to parties, conventions

invitations to speak at lectures
lunch with the President at the White House
and appearances on popular TV show

Groupies beat down your door,
and all your friends envy you

You sleep well at night
never miss a meal
servants at your beck and call

You are in complete control
of your senses, your every emotion,
your surroundings
and your
mind

Yes,
poets
have it
easy

You never have
relationship problems
if your lover gives you trouble,
you just dump them and choose
from the myriad of replacements that lie in wait
and they're all
terrified of losing you

You have steady hands
and solid nerves;
nothing perturbs you

There are no escapist tendencies since,
everything is
already beautiful

I bet I don't know one single poet
who uses chemicals or behaves suicidally

Folks like that
just don't
get rattled

or institutionalized

Yes,
poets
have it
easy

You don't dine with roaches;
you drive nice cars, never have to say please
and you certainly never have to ask

"Can I crash on your couch for a few days?"

"It's only for one more week."

"It's only for one more month."

No

You never have to beg, steal or borrow
you certainly don't sleep in the street
or even in uncomfortable circumstances,
for that matter

You loan money
and don't even worry about it being repaid
you offer one of the many guest rooms to your pals

Everyone simply overlooks
any eccentricities or flaws in your personalities...

Oh, excuse me
that should have been
singular:

personality

Not that you'd ever
have any flaws;
you know,

being a poet
and all

The only work you ever have to do is...
every once in a while...

make something up

Just sit down
in front of your expensive,
state of the art computer
and spit out some gibberish
that sounds
halfway
interesting

Of course,
it's always good insurance
to make it sound
familiar;
you know,
reminiscent
of other poets

But throw some of your own garbage in
so that they'll say

"It's SO
original!
A truly unique
voice!"

Yes,
Poets
Have it
Easy

About the only real nuisances are the constant,
never-ending barrage of fans pestering you
for autographs and begging you to let them
treat you to dinner and so on

And the fact that you're always
on call with your boss,
the Muse

You *do* have to answer Her calls
because She's the one that keeps
all that money rolling in

But honestly,
how bad is that?!
I mean, She's super hot
and She's got the sexiest voice ever heard
It's just got to be a breeze working for Her
She's got class, right?
She's got *real style*

I just can't imagine Her
interfering with your life in any way,
not for something as trivial
and simple as dropping off
a little bit of art to you

It's not like She's going to
grant you inspiration by waking you up at 4 am
insisting that you grab a pen right then and there

Nah, I'm positive She must have a full schedule
you'd have to book an appointment with Her
an important figure like that?
you'd have to book like,
weeks in advance

She's not cruel
it isn't like She's going to
inspire you by getting you fired
or insisting that you pay attention to some idea
when there's something else
that you're supposed to be doing
or something that you just *want* to do

It's not like the Muse hands out inspiration for poetry
by
having friends betray you
or by putting you through tragic events

I mean, that would be
kind of shitty,
wouldn't it?

All those broken relationships and failed ventures
all those missed opportunities that poets
are always droning on about...

I'm sure the Muse just gave them
the ability to *imagine* all of that

and afterward,
the poet and the Muse
probably sat and chatted

over a nice cup of herbal tea
about the next book tour,
cover art and royalties

That's got to be how it is
I mean, seriously...
have you ever seen a poet
hungover, strung out, hungry,
or crying?

I mean, they're always so... fit
well-dressed
and calm

Yeah...

Poets
Have it
Easy

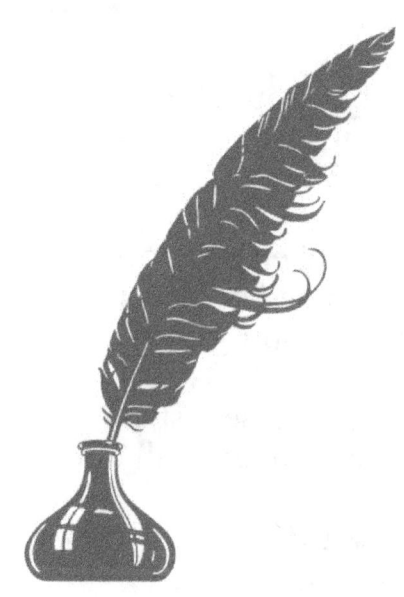

At First Glance

I have no problem imagining
someone might read
one
of my poems
and extrapolate that
all the rest of them
were not worth reading
because of...

pick a reason

however, I can't help but think
that they would want to read
at least
one more

just to see
if they were all...

so terribly strange

but then, I guess
there are other folks
smarter than myself
who would tell you

that's exactly how
you get suckered
into any trap

no poet is without honor, save on his own planet

I had ten million things to say, and I swear,
they were all important

from here on,
please forward your telegraphed punches
to my p.o. box

the local denizens are haggling over beat-up shoes
from the dumpster behind the dollar store

I hear the homeless shelter
is giving out Rolex watches

I fail to understand all of these
invisible partitions
between our smiles

I think I'll invent an inventor
one who will come up with devices
that will solve problems
that we haven't run into yet

perhaps it will invent a contraption
which will retrieve all of my
lost thoughts

or something
that can settle
all these
heated disputes
over frazzled
footwear

plan

Triangulate sweat
Sound the figuring-out siren
Ironing staunch iron
Into the brow of resolve
Turn the map keycode
Crank the shiny ignition
Launch the grits, eggs, and coffee
For a puzzle to solve

Trouble is never too sleepy
To slip up and flank you
It's happy down, muddy
In the trench river blood
Kicking spit into the bruised eye
Doesn't even say thank you
So spank it and hammer it
Into the corner, with a thud

Let the dour enemy go smirking,
Rail against your bright armies
Though shrinking in courage,
Rise defiantly to fight
Swivel the turrets 'round
Aim the win missiles
And know yourself as champion
In dawn's tender first light

That Says It All

Blank pages.

Disappointment.

Learn to appreciate.

The preceding *was not*

A.   An experiment to find out
     How long you would look at nothing
     To find something

B.   A cheap, insincere attempt at art

However, it *may have been*

C.   A challenge to absorb
     More meaning
     From less content

D.   A sincere yet failed attempt at art

The preceding comments
Are hereby stricken from the record.
They will be disregarded.

You must now operate under the assumption
That none of this ever happened.

(Pretend you're a juror)

poets

poets
are lazy writers

they don't have the gall
for a novel
or even
a short story

all they can do is
fart out
a few disconnected feelings
with no structure, storyline,
or flow about it

i say this all the time

of course,

i am a poet
and so,
there must be
something
more
to the
story

that
i have
not
included

Misquoted

What you gonna say,
That will make it thru tday
                    unskaythed
        by tyme   and
                              ill design?

the minds uv men
will "clean up"
your mistakes
oversites, as they see them

they will help to convay
the "true meening"
of your words

don't worry,
they'll take
good care
of your
orijinal intenshuns

really. their good peeple.

                even if you put it
                        a   d
                        p   o
            o   e   w
            n   r   n
                                        p
                            it will comeu

retal tnereffid

17

new poem.

(catchy title, huh?)

poetry
is a liscense
to comit
just about
any
hanous crime.

magnetism

[done with a magnetic poetry kit
on some girl's refrigerator]

we spray languid fluff
as apparatus friends
rock and eat the diamond beat
                    falling water
                              honey
                                tiny knife

a purple gift

          has size

              though urge symphony

                  will still pound the chant

after a moment
an essential
delicate smear
incubates the watch puppy

small words

so i guess this is where i say something
really profound, wise, and insightful

i'm just going to skip that part

pinge, burge... pinge, burge...

nothing new

a stranger called it penance
          and asked if i was catholic

common
fucking junkie
can't kick
small words
into a wastebasket

trial and error
hung jury

efficacious
disease
knees

you know
the drill
assume
the position

jabberwocky flippant hurt
never tasted so good

Improv

Improvement makes straight roads;
but the crooked roads,
without improvement,
are the roads of genius.

—William Blake

It makes very little

Why yes, I do!

Until you spare yourself
The undertow of perfection

Finding the sands of acceptance
Much warmer
More free-flowing
Than glacier

ah, creation!!

let the tea steep
let the ideas stir
let the head wind up
let the typer hum
let the tubes warm
let the music walk and breathe

let the women be beautiful
let the investments mature
let the children grow
let the people be free

let the dancers dance
let the fighters fight
let the games be kept friendly
let the affairs of others go unnoticed

    let the demons who are hunting you
          be damned

    let the strength and innate kindness in your
          heart flourish

let the fish sparkle in the waters
let the gators have the swamps
let the joke be on all of us

let everyone have it as easy
    as you can give it to them

let the intricacies of your mind amaze you

let the humility of the wise deter you
    from speaking that amazement

let the volcanos die and go numb
let the tractors grow weeds underneath

let parliament have all the power; funkadelic, that is

let the pope eat his hat on friday
let the cows stay out late

let the spaghetti westerns speak to you
       as transcendent illumination

Ooops.

When I first started writing poetry
I had read
very little
of the classics,
only what I had
come across
in school

To me, most of the "classics"
were very
foreign
distant
not at all relatable

except for one
small batch
that I tore out
of a high school textbook

There, I met my new friends,
the real, cool kids

Don Marquis' *archy hears from mars*
Rudyard Kipling's *If*

Emily Dickinson, in all of her
unknown brilliance

Edwin Arlington Robinson,
sharing with me the stories of
Miniver Cheevy and *Richard Cory*

and my high school sweetheart,
Sylvia Plath

I was not normally one to
deface textbooks

but then, I didn't want to
leave my friends behind

I still have them today

by the time I started
reading great poets,
geniuses
like Dylan Thomas,
e.e. cummings, Stephen Crane,
Charles Bukowski,
Robert Frost
and dozens of other
superb writers

I had already written
several books worth of
my own poetry

I then realized...

I had
nothing new
to say

It was all just a
re-hash of them,
even though I had never read them

so much
for my grand
contribution
of genius...

of course, by then
I was already entirely too
attached
to my work
and to the art
of writing itself

I was too attached
to go back and
change anything

but I would sometimes wish
that either...
I had never
read those poets

or that I had
never written
anything
of my own

but neither
of these thoughts
was genuinely
honest

and anyway,
by then...

it was
too
late

sugar

she was like the tiny, little

broken, china teacup

that i would use to dip sugar

from out of the big jar

that i kept in the fridge

she was there,

all covered in sticky sweetness...

chipped, jagged

cold

and poised

to cut the lip

Visa

I have stories I want to tell
about events that have not yet happened
futures that I can see only in my mind

I am stitching them slowly
into realities

I have stories I want to tell

sulfurous venting of volcano

waiting quietly for permission
waiting for the muse
to dispense payment,
put that direct deposit into my account

lay the diadem of miracle
upon the brow

tied to delayed blessings

bestowing
unfolding gift
mystery and intrigue

bind words
intoxicating
blue threads
of desire

know

boundless
confidence

I have stories

in need

of a
good
coat

brilliant green

presentable

heard

check is
good

clears the
bank

sir,
your passport is

ready

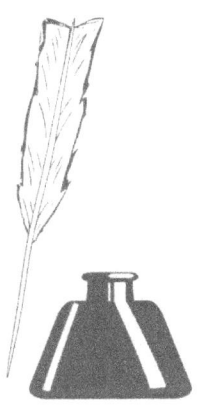

Still On Pause

It's hard to find a place
To keep your memories
I came to the crest of forever
The edge of the wheel
Far gone

In search of things
That I held in my hand
A palace of grandeur
Stands in a land

A far off way from here
A man with cool,
Candied celebrations

A Thought Not Worth Writing Down

Do writers read their own work
In their next lifetimes?

When musicians record albums,
Will they enjoy the entertainment they created
In future incarnations?

Do the builders of homes
Ever reside in those same homes,
The next go around?

if you want to be a poet

inspired by gary snyder's
what you should know to be a poet

i'll tell you
what little
i know:

you must be rich
without money

you must concern yourself
with sensual caresses
whenever possible

you wander
aimlessly,
pointlessly

waiting on buses
waiting in lines
waiting for the muse
waiting for yourself
to catch up
with yourself

you must revel
in the majesty of irony

you must be able to put words
to those things
that others can
describe only
with touch, kisses
laughter, fists, tears

sharpen your wit
by rubbing against
those who are
smarter
than you;
know well
that the number of these
is legion

hand copy a dictionary

then start on the thesaurus

have a good rhyming dictionary

always,
and i mean always,
have pen and paper
cocked and loaded

you will roll and tumble
through sweaty
august mornings,
wondering why it is
that you cannot sleep,
when you have already not slept
for some godawful amount of time

learn the language of language

not so much *the rules*
(which are important)

but the *feeling* and *form* of language;
the art of teaching words
how to caress one another
and explode into each other

read only what inspires you;
not what is merely popular
passed off as being good
by marketers and mindless throngs
of sycophantic yes men fans

yes, ten million people can be
and *frequently are*
wrong

never sacrifice a good idea or a line
only because it isn't a technically proper rhyme

you will lose lovers
family, friends, yourself

most of all, yourself

you will replace them,
sometimes carefully
other times, indiscriminately

you will lose your mind
unless you have already bargained it away
to some country god charity lover cause drug
in which case, your talents will be
lackluster, at best

poetry requires
the blood sacrifice of
virgin mind

keen, sharp, brimming with
constant, new
effervescent ideas
ever-broadening, flowing

and if
for any reason

you fail
to master

simultaneously

the arts of *unshakeable self-esteem*

and *genuine humility*

then just know that
the former is
important

while the latter is

absolutely requisite

now, run along
and read
mr. snyder's piece

which is far, far
better

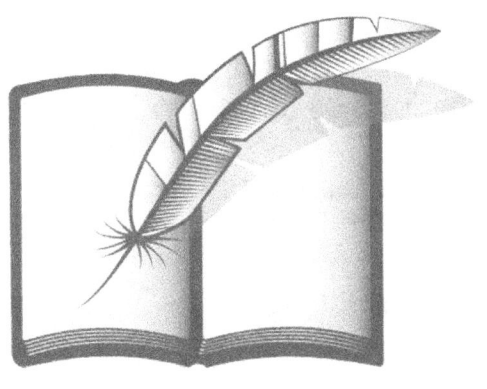

Suicide

Come in
Suicide

Take the couch
Reside a while

Chat with me

But don't you get too comfy

I believe I'll be

      Hanging

In there

For at least
One or two
More

No, I don't believe that today
I'll be needing your services

My own life, I will not break
There is history for me to make
There are bows I've yet to take
That privilege is one I'll not forsake

Come back next week
I may need you then
For now,
My work is
Calling

untitled

When at least your feathers fall
When your hopes at most could only hope to crawl
When all your failures rub you raw
When you're on the ground, tongue in jaw
Do not beg nor whimper nor fold, for I saw
You, when you used to kick and scratch and claw
And for you, there was no match

I have no seeds to spare, nor plant nor save
With good intentions, I already gave
To others that they might have some more
Now winter has come and taken the store
Never surrender your ground but rather
Continue to hunt, grow, toil, and gather
Accolades that I would have you catch

I expect only your best; no such beast as perfection
I've seen you turn wrath in your enemy's direction
Crumbling them, drawing them down to your feet
Where hard, with sudden humility, they meet
So now, with haste and want of hesitation
Rebuild your temple of sacred elation
Burn out their eyes
With the dazzling light of your history

Blow the clamorous trumpet,
Your joyous song of conquest
So loud the sound that none would ever dare to test
Raise high, once again, the proud flag of your might
Let its shadow block the sun and cover all moonlight
Conclude all tired works of a flagging, sad day
The early tomorrow has something wonderful to say
Nothing less than
A holy proclamation of your victory

Stake Out

sitting here on the curb, in front of the bank
I think every passerby can tell
that I just spent my last two bucks
on a candy bar, a small bag of chips, and a generic
soda

they can see the depth of my debt;
right through my empty pockets

I'd need a job that pays a hundred dollars an hour
just to catch up to zero

I must look very suspicious, sitting here
these desperate eyes, all aflame
with a hot, compulsory need

you see, I'm a street musician
and if you will only put
a few dollars in my instrument case,
it might keep me away from firearms
and out of your banks

maybe

I just need enough to eat, occasionally
and to buy guitar strings

> *"please, mister banker,*
> *won't you do this thing for me?"*

you might consider
dropping some cash into my case
and writing it off
as insurance

untitled

I.

i used to believe
now i know
i can still show you a smile
look how it glows
i know everything
is happy and blissful

what's the matter?
you don't believe me?
that's ok

i will prove it to you...
right across your skull

there.
now do you see it?
yes? excellent.
i knew you would.
see now?
that wasn't so bad,
was it?

II.

beauty is the best trap
that one can devise

and a solid alibi
should questions arise

drop

capability
to understand

to understand
capability

insufferable acuity

possibility of escape
not easily grasped
discombobulated
by pin drop

cannot undo
wanton,
useless thing

awful, thudding ache
in thoughtless regions

stomach
a more reliable
sourcing of
informed decisions

thought
audibly heard

evocative commentaries
delivery of powerful
unfolding implications

actions
grown used to neglect
speech ignored

those who speak
no forethought
into the lap

gnawing at the solar plexus
center
energy and intellect

acidic
contrived
efficiency

drop

drop of blood
in the throat

drop words
unbreakable

priceless things

broken
in the process

sound

overcomes

matter

What's On?

If thoughts and distance are able to measure
the size of your mind
and how far you see
then I'd best keep myself
confined to within about ten feet
of the TV

Poetry is pain
and I a poet
my doldrum scrolls
for all to see
but I'll prop myself up
in front of the tube
let it cure
my despondency

Koan

Existence is not difficult for those who make no discriminations.

  —Zen Koan

Everything in life is dangerous. What's the point of being afraid?

  —some drunk guy at the bar who thought he had scared me away with his rambling but I really just needed to piss

The world no longer frightens me. I'm not scared anymore. It just disappoints me. Itallrunstogether likewetpaintonaparkbench onahotsummersday and I just don't want to be here anymore.

  —what I would have said to my friend, had I not been so sure that it would have frightened him

What's your name? You're very pretty.

  —what I said to the girl on the street with the small dog

Oh, thanks. Bye.

  —what she said as she hurried away

When you can do nothing, what can you do?

  —Zen Koan

it's just poetry

it's just poetry

don't sweat it
just read it
look at it
see it

hear, feel, taste... *know*

try to get
something
out of the
experience

well,
not exactly *try;*
don't *try*

just try
by *not trying*

when I say
get something out of it...

I mean something
relevant to
you

not necessarily
something deep
or enlightening
just something
that means something
to you

ok, so I can't exactly
describe
this *thing*

that's because
it's not my thing
and it never
will be

it's yours

it's ok
if you don't
know
what it is
yet

you'll know it
when you
see it
or
hear it

if you never do...
see it or hear it

don't fret

it's just
poetry

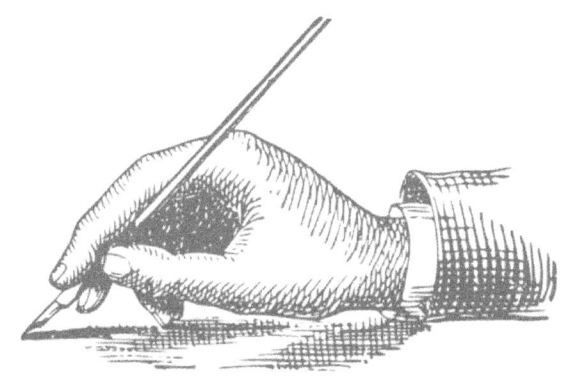

you wouldn't know

you wouldn't know you were alive
if you tripped over your soul

you are afraid

success

feathers fly
full quill
empties
in my direction

you were never pushed
in any direction
except the one you begged for

still,
you strike
subconscious
jealousy

you know that
sooner...
later

I make it
past
the wire

you
will not

self-sabotage

all your brilliant ideas
keep me
in line

tantrum
all good

soap opera extra credit assignments
children
telling stories

as for me, I have not the time
nit-picking perfectionist
procrastination
ne'er do well genius
nothing ever
good enough
and so,
nothing

waiting around for
everything

deliveries to doorsteps
red bows
tied
on top

will not...
that this was ever...
me

with you, there is always
something
not quite...
and so, with you...
there is nothing

excuse me now
excuses for
me

make a run past the wire
get past the guard

into world of the living

sorry, no new reconnaissance reports today

crabs in the picnic basket
pulling back
down

no more a part
in Greek tragedy

insisting on hero

pick up
where
father left

hometown neighbors
failure

the having of whole
huge, impossible
astronomical
odds

a thing going on

cherished
nemesis

no more tripping
treading uncomfortable coffee

tread over
trap

go around

door between worlds
slams

damned

damn

not enough
perdition

no sharing

ball up wads of newspaper
one of my old shirts

pretend

still have
someone
to complain

after

a pinch of madness

insane notions of a poet, sorcerer
a singer of peculiar songs
rhythmic, vain ideation
one who conjured strange creatures
from the cauldron of creation

over and beyond this threshold
you partake of leisures
sound and sultry syllable
lessons, lectures, laughters
the lesions of wounded minds,
weary with the weight of life
giddy with the youthful joys
of the coil-sprung death instrument
cosmos and its temporal, jittery stasis

tune in to mad frequency of the hatter's harp
feel feathery quill between your fingers,
scratching soft illusions of underworld cathedrals
onto digital parchment, binary scrolls of data
into thousand, orb-like eyes of the argus

place your nefarious left hand into nebulous,
darkened grab bag
of glasslike candies and venomous serpents

here, you will know not, quilted comforts of certainty
only gambler's thrill, wanton abandon
mercurial mirth whispered into ear

tipping for the tune, speaking of the rhyme
receive the song, bartering the verse of a dime
witch ways abounding in universe of sound

words walk here like men
men speaking lessons
instructions in the arts
summoning demons

demons who cut
doorways in the daylight

doors through which only angels may pass

angels entering into the earth
making oddly-perfumed flowers
flowers blooming
children
revisiting all birth
under
cold rocks
of winter

children who spend their time
slaughtering gods for sport
beautiful, terrible gods
that bleed dying stars

stars
using up all
last, tortured
breath

spitting
dust
and
light

you

untitled

I.

The goodness is where?
Of here, it is changed
If ever it was anything,
It is different now

II.

When the cubes keep popping out
What's a glass homeowner supposed to do?
Other than twist them back into place
With a screwdriver?

These jobs are hell in the hot morning sun

III.

You know why we drink

It is an art all but lost
And no one listens

People who live
In paper houses
Should not throw poems

untitled

the world demands of you a purpose
your useful skill, they'll want to know
even if only a bricklayer or a criminal
you must have something profitable to show

they'll pardon the old and children
but never those... *other folks*
they'll shoot the poets for wantonness
unproductive outsiders, always cracking jokes

they'll pardon those with lots of money
since they have something valuable to lend
myself, I'll surely end up on the gallows
with no gold for the hangman to spend

We Miss Things

We miss things

Something
Through
Every
Other
Over
Time

So close, so far

Cycling on elusive axis
Groped at
Escapes

Feel a change in the pressure and direction
In the infinite waters
Embryonic womb
As a cosmic symmetry
Swims right on by
Missed
Narrow margin

Crucial connection
Slip from the grasp

Could have
Brought it all back
Together
Still sweating
In the turmoil

A far gone closeness
To what is sought

Through, Over Something,
Every Other
Time

Serpent passover for children
Hiding in game rooms
Clutching at loose garments
Slipping away
Turning furiously
Wheels
Bring back the water
Wash it all away

Over Every Something,
Through
Other,
Time

Laughter shaming progress
Bring painful awareness
Of waxen images;
Makes us silly,
Makes us miss things

Through,
Every Something,
Over,
Time

Vibrant chords ring
Central nervousness

Deafening tones
Internal instruments
Age old

Storing up starved babies

For the winter
Preserving in quarantine;
What can
In cans
Only sour

Majesty in mason jars
Admired
Only through the glass

Through Something,
Over,
Every Other,
Time

Nursing the young
Curdled milk of fear
Warm harbor of silence
The bray of stubborn ass
Alongside peace and wisdom

Sanity slips out
Quiet
Careful door slams
Makes us miss things

Every
Time
Something
Other
Over
Through

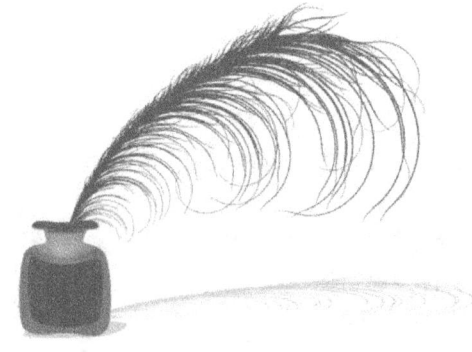

shine

it is not for me
to shine

rays, dispersing
shadow, reveal
only trifles

inciting war

fire falls
on fuses,
short

endless
ill will
abounds

and yet,
the light
escapes

from any
and all
attempts
to contain

victories

sitting
with books

initial investigations
provocative

promising
perhaps

after
devotion

patient
time

energy
left

feeling
cheated

stuffed rehash
earlier failures

vulnerability
sly marketing
technique

malleable
sucker
no wonder
so many...
lost
gone

done

down

into
the
tube

hot glass
incinerates
all

paper
obsolete

some

absolution

trudge on

recommend

victories

afterward

each piece settles snugly once more
into what is acceptable boundaries
                    of reality

plush pools of familiar
        carpentry

bar stools and friendly
        pageantry

door posts suffering
        valiantly

to suspend much-needed roofs
        above our stormy weather

gather us together

and gather together, we will

when the centuries
are stuffed into the frame
the shape of an hour
—resembling an accordion—
for the purpose
of listening

The Bricks of Lonely Night

I.

Requirement of sitting
Occasional doldrums of rubble pile
Mandatory;
No exceptions

Night's unique gift
Stacking solid, black bricks
Up
High
Tired eyes too weak to penetrate
Camouflaged hope

Eating gutter leaves of gutless dusk
All soggy with autumn mold
No rockstar breakfast cereal
Career of envisioning the icing
Slathering it on life's cake

Spending the all afternoon,
Learning the strange braille of concrete
Making casual quips of weather discussion
With the neighbor's dog
Arguing whether caterpillar
Will cross over
Or go back
Into the tall grass

And with a whoosh, all is up and evaporated
The whole long complete total day...
Poof.
Gone, annihilated by sun's magnifier glass
Burnt crispy clock watch

Timepiece toast
All its coercive schemes
Clueless
Where is that confounded, forgotten day?

Perhaps on the subway cab car bike seat
In other backpack briefcase purse wallet

Glamorous work
This gargantuan weight of waiting
For nights
Fog dissolving in the pan
Turning up flame
Scorch the butter
Attempts to accelerate the visage
Of splendor

Catch the small glimmer...

This, the best of crumbling advisory tactics
Scrounged by mad hatter
From beneath lost pretzels and cereal bits
Down, in furry underside
Of counseling couches,
Heavy with old magazines and sadness

Still,
Under wise control
Tedious, tugboat trawler's crawl
Sails just fine,
All weary tired daunted though it is
Sagging, perhaps
A bit low in the water

Some days
Simply
Outnumbered

Assailants of trouble
Masked desperados of duplication
Expensive, gold plated anchors of duty
Dreariness dependents
Self-imposed exiles
Wrath of wrong places
Even more inopportune timings

Eventually, we may discover
Alabaster wonder awaits
Over the peak
Obscured by storm clouds
One or the other

Package deal
They will not sell you
The burger without the fries

Somewhere in that gypsy forrest,
Lined with Mother of Pearl and rubies
Dancing, as it does
Upon the sullen heads
Of even the worst of days

Odometer lies
Time elapsed photos
All grabby
Trying desperately to connect

Gluing us into those magnificent slots
Eager rivets
Tacking thumb notices
Into celebration's cork board
Don't forget us

Nail driven slowly into that dense hardwood
Triumphant moments

The shiny photo
Glamorous center-aisle display box
Promises of the each and every one

Surprise party waiting
A friend's mother
Fresh, gooey batch of your favorite cookies
Dish nearly tumbling down off the table
Reaching for you
Baby cries for mama, stretching
Flexing tiny, fat fingers in distress

Shining radiant bliss waits in the back
Tailor patiently sitting in his booth
Ready to fit garments for the event
Christmas suit of passionate perfection
Cloth tape hanging around his neck
Old, beat-up pair of cloth scissors snarls
Eagerly prepping
Chomping at the ticking minutes

Miles have their nasty habits
Falling in between us and
Picturesque champion snapshots of glory

Trophies offer not much
In the way of conversation
Long, sharp nights of excess acuity
Reeling in awareness of an ever-lengthening longness
All those orangish-yellow highway lines
The gaudy rudeness with which they
Fling themselves under your flying feet
Hundreds of thousands of ugly lemmings
Ready to die beneath a four-door sedan

Nothing gained from it,
Save forcing one to endure that same,

Excruciating song on the jabbering radio
Followed by the same crippling commercials
Looping around the space-time continuum
A nightmare of hair-pulling boredom

Stupid, this
Sitting powerless in the dust
Caressing piles of broken memory
Glancing at the mocking clock
Hoping for daylight to break the spell
Of lonely night

Stupid, requisite

Powerful in its ability to render
Even the mostest giantest, gianty giants
Suddenly all still and sullen
Under the beheading behest of supreme strength
Feeling the loss of connection
Gained by lost breakfast talks with dead friends
Important meetings with the who's who
One begins to toss around certain words
Headache terminology
Existential crisis

Reaching for the affection of those
Who scrambled out time's back window,
Early last year, on a Friday afternoon at 9:30 am

Precise time recalled, only because
It was a Tuesday evening, and you remember because
Your favorite show was howling in the background

Suddenly they shot into peripheral vision
There to howl and drown
Lonely at the bottom of time's unkempt,
Moldy backyard swimming pool

All those forgotten eyes
Staring up from oblivion
Glued now to picture frames and headlines

We bury the dead

They do not always bury us
Now and again
They come 'round to call

Make a strong cup of distraction
Stack another pancake and stack them well,
A wall of syrupy joyfulness that will make
The other-all-every-ones jealous
For the delightful experience of... being you
That special one who lives without inconvenient

Pause

II.

Full of perpetual glow, your precise gears
Grinding always, working away
But each clawing gash in the metal
Made by that ferocious grinder
Brings you closer to that realized bliss that is
Your every waking moment

But pancakes settle, don't they?
After that bloated, comatose napping fit
They fold up and rout off, defeated
Cringing and retreating
Somewhere into the nether, night regions
Of intestinal jungles

Down into the dimly lit belly of Earth
Where the shaman sits,
Quietly smoking the pipe of his
Jaguar and monkey knowledge

Wisdom of knowing
That night and night, alone
Is all

There is nothing else inside the monster
The beast is us, and we are the night
Night waits for the monkeys and jaguars
And it waits for you and for he and I to join it
In that sorrowful song
Deep Egyptian blue silence

Night waits... a most patient hunter
Calm and unhurried, cool and collected
We sing through it in our peculiar registers
Octaves unique to each
All hitting their respective high notes
With fervor, in tune, and on time
Getting bored and sloppy during the
Less exciting, supporting harmonies

Time, ticking away boredom's beat
With its heavy sticks and heavy mallets
Of inescapable truths and reruns on TV

Clicking away at devices, blinking boxes,
Deliberate and flashing

Purporting their falsehoods of Yellow Brick Roads
Where titans are said to be
There, on golden thrones
Drinking the sweet wine of all that is...
Just outside of reach

Some days, time's vast army
Falls fiercely upon our dry throats
With slow slices of sameness
Forcing into rebellious, defiant brows
Painful blades of realization
It's garbage day,
Again

Stack the refuse of soon gull fine dining
In the hot stench of landfill wanting
Revel in the cool, deadpan reliability of small chores

Optimistically grasp for the heart of fun
Sticking your head into that Halloween tub
Of bobbing caramel apple pie candy cakes
Purposefully scoping enjoyment
With crack-shot sniper aim

Feeling for... dive deep for bits of satisfaction
Feels as if... never to be had, found, spoken of...
Again

Resurface disappointed
Coming back up with a mouthful of dust

Oh, you will dance again,
Fair angel of the prom disco ball banquet

But until the morrow rings you up at 9 am,
With that new contract and all its glitz...
You will sit here with the rest of us
Each by ourselves, alone
Even in great numbers and accompanied by
Highly sought after types of company

You will sit with us here, mute and questioning
How not one of these two-ton bricks

Adds not even the tiniest slurp from the dregs
Of a smidgeon's teaspoon ounce of interest
However hard we squeeze and milk that dead horse
For curiosity's nectar

More rotting buffet buckets
Tomorrow's immense, black storm clouds
Ravenous flocks
Foul tempered birds

Some days stretch into nights
Haphazardly falling into the nun's habits
Of long, penitent novenas
In weeks of nights of years of wanting

Wanting for the less-wilting enthusiasm
Clapping for the genie who grants the good time
Galavanting gumdrops,
The ones that used to fall so easily
Out of your prom tuxedo and wedding dress
The little mints you find in old jacket vest coat pockets
After being taken out to dinner
To celebrate your new promotion graduation nuptials

Some days pop you; sucker punch quick
Right in the never-expecting jaw
With electric kung fu cattle prod
Waking from the stun,
Wondering where that day crawled off to
Passed out in the hedgerow of bushes,
Like the town drunk seeking a secret spot
To sleep off all the anger swallowed
Dream on, resilient force
Springy, bounce-backness

Tomorrow is only faking its absence
It hides beneath a bed,

Propped up by a crumbling brick
Memory insists, with all the potent force of a king
Submit and lie down again
In the distant, gone far emptiness of night

Where all men and women and children
Dogs and caterpillars and seagulls
Jaguars and monkeys and men and monkey men
Are laid still in their soft, comforter deaths
Of awakened watching for new light
Pining for hope, like the miserly, morsel crumb dogs
That each of us truly is

Lie still, in your covers, and be content to
Fall into that frightening, eternal well of dark
It slides down a strange white rabbit tube
Into splintering dawns of inexhaustible possibilities

Funny, how beneath the wagon load
Of all these dusty rectangles
We find the means of rebuilding empires

We lift heavy, cloudy eyes
Reddened by lust for things that we know nothing of
We forget to see
We wrestle with the easel
That supports night's blank canvass
Unsettling, that blank slate
Creeps up the brain, with its uneasy feels
Chalky ineptitude, wavering stupid
Failing to answer the teacher's question,
Although it was the first to raise its eager hand

As we wrestle with the easel,
More of the picture, we block with our hands
More of the brush strokes of dawn's fresh paint
Obscured by fat, fumbling impatience

Know that you will not dance tonight,
You kings and queens of the prom

Tonight, you will curse the mild meal
And the mute telephone
You will stare blankly at the lack of...
Anything and everything

But if you listen astutely to time's tepid song,
You might, however briefly, hear your name called out
Incredibly quietly, precisely on time

For the night, which has swallowed us up whole
(Biblical whale belly that it is)
That same night, which shows you nothing
But discontent...

It is the same panoramic, paranoid landscape of
Empty, absence of light that engulfs each of the others
In all their vainglorious retellings
Of the evening's accomplishments
For they, as well, lose their ruby slippers at midnight
Tear their gowns and retreat home
To brush their teeth and take out the trash
To feed the dogs and cats and seagulls
They, too, climb into the warm bath
Full of wine and the valium of television

Finally, the snug wrap of darkness
Its pile of crumbling memories
Stacking higher around them each
Passing eternity of ever and ever
Until they crash suddenly into morning

Let go and dive deep
Somewhere, in the subterranean tubes
Of midnight's stale crackers and tea

There lies the fluffy, white bunny
Erratic and mad and full of terminal flurries
Calculated calendars
Eager, always on to the next

Softly, your name falls into his long, furry ears
With their destiny of long listening
For tomorrow's timely whistles...

If you are quiet and do not disturb the black curtain
In all of its agitated equilibrium
Then the rabbit will whisper your name
Just as time has
Whispered its strange secrets, unto him

And that sparkling sound,
Which is your very own appellation,
Will ring the bell of church mouse chimes
Of morning's birds, chirping in new daylight
With all its bright and equal obliviousness

You will be awake to chase your odd bunnies
Through their well-lit insanities
Until at last, exhausted and fumbling
Through the ruined civilizations of
Afternoon's crumbling sunlight cathedrals
Their tumbling, tired bricks of busyness

You will alarm even yourself
As you become aware of that odd, new sound
Which is your mouth, doing what must be
An imitation of some other strange foreign imposter
Allowing the escape of seemingly absurd
Mad prisoner words

Tousle with the body snatch invader notion
Of demon possession, since it must be some devil

Who puts forth this blasphemous heresy
Making it seem as if you, yourself
Uttered the sin...

A crisp and brief prayer
For the serenity and slumber
Of having just one,

Solitary, calm
Quiet, eventless
Night

blank slate

brain is full of dust
chalkboard remnants
memory
slate wiped clean
lack of sleep

whiteout
bad term paper editing
mayonnaise spread over burnt toast
a fresh coat of whitewash
sugar cookie mind,
dunked in whole milk
deliciously unstable

6:22 am no flag yet on the purple horizon
home base
invisible

no clicking crunchy keys with which to
enter that soft place
enveloped in the sweet smells
of baby's hair and women's perfumes
fairground of a thousand amusements
no lines to wait in

I tap on boxes of light
for the passing time

one makes pictures move
captures the easy prey
my dazed attention

the other moves crystal armies
across theoretical landscapes

much like those, I walk, daily
and call my world

it is I who wins, as often as it is not
and none of it is of any real consequence
nothing comes of any of it

much like those situations, I live, daily
and call my life

wonder the portent of trivial distraction

6:28 blank

out

caress musical companion
dog sleeps beneath the covers
keeping the woman warm

here sits one,
burning candles
at more ends
than candles possess,
according to the legends
of candles
and their ends
and the stories of those
who burn

I am immensely thankful
for the tiny bits of nothing
that I cannot remember

Poetry Sundays

poetry, on Sundays
where I reside

smoking
drinking
talking
smiling
at nothing

sometimes, someone will
read a poem

sometimes, belligerence
spills out of my rock glass
and starts raving on about
how things ought to be

as if I knew any better on the matter

a friend asked if my complaint was
lucidity or just discontent

I asked, "What's the difference?"

I take a particular, small delight
in demolishing sandcastles
as do we all, but I prefer first
to build them up, strong and tall
give them a time to stand, shine

I wait until they have become entirely too small
for my ever-expanding,
opulent, rockstar,
millionaire lifestyle

before I demolish them for something grander;
oddly enough, this takes far more time
than you might imagine
so many know nothing except how to destroy

destroying a thing to make way for a new, better thing
this... divine precedent, evolution

to destroy a thing
for the mere pleasure of destroying it
offering nothing new to replace it
this... premature ejaculation, stupid precarious
faltering larceny
indehiscent schoolyard abominations
tossing firecrackers into metal trash cans for sport

majesty hides in potential unions
ear and orator locked in a mental, soft screw

Jacob's Ladder
leaned up against the Tower of Babel

trying to get into heaven
failing due to condition
of being

something potent in the hand
balls of opium, sweet and intoxicating
keys to palaces of pleasure

flung thoughtlessly away...
a child's finger, flicking boogers

power of words
worthy
those emissaries of the sway

unhappy ignorance
hovers over
tongues of indifference
speak to yourselves of restraint
a good lashing
of leather tongues

come to multiple come to Jesus meetings
melodramatic soap opera scripts
left on the cutting room floor

sloppy language
vocabulary of the moon
subconscious walks
three feet ahead at all times
announces every movement

opportunity to know
things best kept to self

off of the chin
hanging
a bit of jelly donut
no one mentions; rude fears

chocolate covered mouths
amuck, through the no sign of mother

malicious diplomacy of craft,
crafting only more diplomacy

words, both art
and arsenal
challenge change,
growing artisans
nurture intellect
a babe

yet to be
invoke that kind
benevolent, old god
the one who gives
good gifts of good discourse

those which are known for lacking
that which is rarely sweet
and less often
true

known as well
for their intentional
incompleteness...

that you
might listen
and be full

and share this fullness
with your brothers and sisters
majesty,
falling out of
your mouths

dripping
from your tongues

words of
honey

A Thousand and One

A thousand silver bowls
    of poisonous mushroom stew
A thousand vital jobs
    without a single thing to do

A thousand glass butterflies
    on a monkey's cold hand
A thousand blades of dead grass
    on a solid gold stand

Each of these, being more sensible
    holding more logical sway
Than the reasons you gave
    when you went away

haiku charades

not indicative
of anything that I know
complete mystery

can someone please give
is there a hint you might show?
I'm failing to see

wild gestures you make
flopping like a fish on land
still, I am confused

nothing is at stake
yet, angrily, you demand
clues already used

almost something like it

you say you've been
to the mountain
and now you're
a big to do

funny
but I don't remember
the mountain
ever mentioning you

I am not your memories

that frame cracked
when I outgrew

shards of recollection
lay strewn about your rug

no mere incomplete reflection
of your patronizing shrug

I am no broken piece of you

I no longer fit
on your wall
or in your wallet

a thousand pardons

a thousand pardons
     for a thousand deeds
             undone

may the night forgive my sin of omission
        my trespass of complacency

a new star rises

     pray to tomorrow

        unexpected campaigns
           on more ordinary fronts
              a more common stage

I have been released from my pregnancy
     by the scavengers of distraction

to conceive again is unthinkable
              and yet...

it is
       as certain
             as the morning

the childless grieve
the newborns breathe

        on and on and on

canned biscuits

season of
mad cash

death of the
middleman

goose flesh
armageddon

revel in it all
and somehow
make it
your own

pinhead jerk-offs
radio blather

excrement

automobile advertising
root of all evil

cut back on
quality

increase
profit
margarine

downsize
personnel
make smaller
people

size up
value
combos

in
but not
of...

contend
with it
all

somehow...
make it

your
own

stain

he was speaking vodka
a language that I all-too-well
understood

as I sat on the edge of his bed,
I handed him the joint
that I had just finished
carefully rolling

he lit it and took a small toke
became suddenly
and uncharacteristically
serious

    "You do know that I'm not life, right?"

it must have been obvious that I had no clue
how to answer that
so he continued...

    "When I was just a little boy,
    your grandpa (and mine) told me...
    he said,

        'Son, you'll pull time
        before you hit twenty.'

    At nineteen,
    I did six months."

before he could say another word,
several drunk people filed into the room
and the party took over

as if the writer of this dark comedy of errors
had carefully placed it into the script
for dramatic effect

about fifteen years later
I stood in the yard
with my father
one morning

we burned a mattress
in the yard

a mattress with a peculiar
red stain
on the top end of it,
right about where a man
would lay his head down
to sleep

smoke climbed through the
bare tree branches
coating the limbs
blackening the sun

giving twisted
new meaning
to the wind

with each searing crackle,
each hot, little iron that launched out
from the flame,
the notion was solidified...

you would not
be here with us
again

that red stain has been
forever removed

taken off and away
from the bad blend of cotton
and synthetic fiber

its ugly, lack of aesthetic
removed from the eye

we have instead
embroidered you
into the heart
in gold-letter, on satin

a little redirection
a simple trick of the firelight
and the mind

a touch of pre-approved
manipulation
vocabulary and memory,
now twisted to suit ourselves
with semblances of sanity

and yourself, in a new suit
one to bring you
over the threshold of the
next beginning,
in a dapper style

we have gathered many flowers
of which you were one

still,
we do so wish

that you
were not so
still

we are so much more
careful now
with our words

before, we never had to
monitor our tongues

we counted on you
to always say something
deliciously profane
hysterical, sublime

something far more terrible
than we would ever manage (or dare)
to bring forth from our own,
fearful mouths

you said it all
for us

being our favorite devil,
you spared no words
knowing full well,
that your time
was short

now it has all fallen
serious and sullen

and ash settles on us
stealing the still-warm seat
of smiles

we do our best
to preserve the integrity
of your memory

with all your words,
so clumsily wrong,
so horribly right

your faults fill volumes
all of these now consumed by fire
and forgetfulness

we will not miss them

we are, in fact, glad to be free of these
free from the weight of your
awful acuity

your condemnation of this world
was felt, always
hot upon our necks

virtually indecipherable
from the indiscriminate joy
that your voice poured out
over our wanting brains
we will not miss the anarchy of your actions
your allegiance to an autocratic indifference

but beneath the intolerable heavy,
knowing of nothing else to do...

we dutifully lift our eyes
to the coming days
where you
are not

emblem

cup bears emblem
of joy

overflowing
with war

crunching sounds
knowledge
beneath
a conqueror's boot

sip quietly
the vessel
of blood

know
simply
nothing
else
to drink

a libation of fire
thirst

choices

sometimes
we label things

accuracy

invisible
target

circa 1929

nothing now but file cabinets and bookcases
and sound;
jazz, as usual

this old house creaks
staying in new places is always weird
having lived in a truly haunted house once before,
I had worried that the
unknown
might occupy this one too

but I have been here now long enough to say
that I am the only one here; I am alone

ironically, this fact comforts me
not at all

yep, it's just me...
and, of course, the rats that scurry
under the foundation

the executioner, with his chemical hatchet,
delivers an untimely end

found lipstick
on one of my old poetry notebooks
(don't ask me how)

just a further reminder of the gulag

I've been sick now for seven hundred forty-six days,
squeezed into three, neat, little, twenty-four-hour
[compartments]

someone always seems to be peering in at me
through the winking hole in my skull;
reminding me that it is
time

time:
to take out the trash
to beat the wolves away from the door
with a thick stick of $$$Money
to take more blu, flu concoction
to think about time

I fill my metal wastebasket
with white flowers of delirium
masterpieces of mucous
balled-up milestones of treacherous misery

I listen to the radio, spewing its vomit
recanting the recent atrocities
that my brothers have committed against each other
accounts of foreign and bizarre deaths
in foreign and mysterious places

but thankfully, those artisans of air:
the invisible jazzmen, who jump out of my speakers;
gleefully chiseling more memorable memorandum
into the membrane of my one, good ear

cool horns blow
gas burns slow and fierce
cold does battle with my window panes
I am fortunate to be inside, indoors
even with broken glass and an old carpet
lying out on my downtrodden lawn

my old but new-to-me shelter from the elements
has a *je ne sais quoi*

that is not so much "old-world charm"
as it is dilapidation,
renunciation, and rejection

as far as decorating schemes go
I've been going for that whole
Salvation Army look
and I think I'm pulling it off quite nicely,
if I do say so myself

but it's a quiet neighborhood
and I can *almost* afford it
at least the place is mine
that is until the lease is up
or they boot me out for not paying my rent

for now, these four walls serve as some sort of
a touchstone of normality or sanity
or any other synonym for boredom

so I'll put patches on the knees
of this ancient pair of dungarees
and go about caulking the windows
or as I like to refer to it:
sand-bagging the trenches for thermal warfare

the painting of walls, cabinets, trim work
eventually, I'll tackle the outside too
a nouveau being has got to keep busy, right?
keep churning that existential angst
or god forbid I might get quiet
and learn something from the stillness

must do something to stave off all that
nauseating samadhi

me?

I listen to public radio and jazz albums
it keeps the bats out of the belfry
or in... I forget

I pay endless slipstreams of final notices
and late fees on the late fees

I conquer seemingly insurmountable difficulties
one at a time,
despite myself

I keep fixing up this dump
prepare it to christen it
a home

I continue to cultivate sound
words and music
stemming from shoots of fresh inspiration
flowers that bloom in the brain

hell...
everybody's
gotta have a hobby,
right?

I'm a musician and a writer
so obviously,
I collect food stamps

rain

i can feel the rain coming
in my spirit

like the old man
in the rocking chair
on his front porch

i feel it in every bone
every trick limb
and aching joint

a sweeping sense of despair
as my head passes through a

deluge

something similar to
a drive through car wash, only...
less convenient

a team of pressurized fire hoses
and enormous, comic pompoms
thwacking me right in my
frontal cortex

as the weather makes its approach,
there's a sweeping sense of despair

as the weather makes its slow, arrogant approach
i know its imminent arrival, often hours beforehand...

before the first cloud ever rears its muddy, black
disapproving face
my bones crack and my hopes
sag

nothing fazes
the stupor

a dark, somnolent plague
of inefficient sleep
brought on by
a simple change of
barometric pressure

a slight swing of

humidity;

a little water

a little water can

drown

my

w

o

r

l

d

never approaching
the front page
ranking only
section c in the newspaper

the c section
opens my skull
and dumps that precious
baby brain on the
cold, tile floor
kicking it into the corner,
near the waste can

those morons at the paper
ought to recognize
that murder is more of a
frontpage deal
they view it as
a little spill on the carpet

it's only water
don't cry

i won't cry,
but i will sleep

i am drugged and stuffed into a canvas bag
by this natural sedative
carted off to the ocean of inactivity
and dumped in
left for dead
with a note pinned to my scalp:

> "you will submit to my dominance
> you will curl up in a soggy, little ball
> and wait for me to pass."

i have survived seemingly intolerable
fires of the spirit
unquenchable flames of the heart
earth scorching plumes of fire
setting daily life alight

i've dealt with dozens of
major catastrophes

not to mention hundreds of
tiny conflagrations

the little fires
that need
putting out

only to be
doused

and completely
extinguished

by

a

little

w
  a
    t
      e
        r

scorpion, fish, eagle

have you learned the ways of war
have you stood on the skull of a dead man
to help yourself up from a trench of blood

have you sung to the sleeping child
stood in the bay window of a woman's heart
admired the sunset
do you know the secret fusion of the sun
dark matter of being
the twilight path of the moon
urchin of the ocean floor

have you been burned
buried thousands of feet
beneath the surface of the earth
swam with magma and danced with plumes of fire
can you recite the names
of the demons you've dined with
the deities
you have swatted down like pestilent flies

has the skin jumped off of your flesh
at the sight of a loved one in peril
have you defended the honor of a stranger
stolen a meager meal from a condemned man
have you plucked out your own eyes
prevented the sight of unspeakable evil
paid a high price just to see the sin

until you have done all of these and none
below the abyss, you will remain
you do well to remember that
art is all that stands between death and the devil
the universe begets the fool
and vice versa

Mind Game

I tell you what I see
Not what I wish to be

Not what you wish to hear me say
No, my friend, it is the other way

I tell you only what I see to be clear
And yet I say this with no fear

But as your thoughts are plainly read
I detect your fear of what I said

I sense the dread; it's in your eyes
The mask of your thinking is a poor disguise

Your reasoning lacks reason
It is a form of self-treason

Hiding truth from one's self is grotesquely bizarre
For when deceiving yourself, you become not who
you are

An enemy to one's being
Never resting, ever fleeing

As was said to me, I say in turn to you
Lie not to yourself; to thine own self be true

restaurants and rough days

there's a loud vacuum cleaner going on
in the coffee house, giving me a headache

i'm drowning my sorrows in a glass of sweet tea
meditating on the fact that i have too much shit
that pawnshops won't take
things like: rejection notices from poetry editors
d.m.v. notices that claim i owe money
parking tickets and love letters from bill collectors;
i have lots of notices

but no one is taking notice of the things
that i want noticed, like:
my art, my music, and my poetry;
i guess it wasn't very noticeable

i'm on the verge of breaking down in tears
in front of perfect strangers
people who would more than likely
respond in an uneasy fashion, at best
and don henley is on the stereo, assuring me

> *"this is the last*
> *worthless evening*
> *that you'll have to spend."*

things would undoubtedly be better
were i in paris, sipping drinks
with some drop-dead gorgeous dame
and whispering in the language of love

don't you dare pipe up and tell me
that nothing would be different;
i already know that

i know you cannot run from your problems
because they'll follow you until you solve them

but you keep your useless trap shut and let me dream

i exist at this moment
solely for this glass of iced tea
and this pack of cheap cigarettes

the waitress is nice, and it's not just for a good tip;
you can always sense these things; at least i can

the air conditioner is blowing hard
and i'm shaking, although i'm not cold
it's just caffeine and high expectations
silly combinations

i love this sweet tea
the waitress, she seems to like me
but she's not coming by as often
i think she can see that i'm upset
probably wouldn't want to embarrass me

maybe i disturb her
maybe that's why she's attracted to me
sweet girl,
brings more tea when i ask

i am steeling myself for the next round of the fight
i am resolving to love this life, in spite of everything

i will sell everything i have to keep myself alive
if that's what it takes
and it appears that this is
precisely what it's going to take
i will starve and beg for it
show people that i love life more than they do

because i starve and beg
to achieve my not-very-noticeable art
instead of selling my hours to the company store
and they will all be oh, so very impressed,
i'm sure

maybe i'll wise up and take stock
of all the good that's right here around me, like:

air conditioning
like the fact that the d.m.v. only wants money from
me
because i still have a car
the fact that i am getting some
much needed attention from a cute waitress

maybe i'll stop whining about the attention
that i'm not getting from people i've never met
like arrogant, tasteless poetry editors

and the unwanted attention i'm getting
from people like bill collectors

someone, somewhere, will recognize the struggle
and appreciate my version of it
someone will notice and offer valuable assistance
or at least some meager approval,
to keep me moving

or maybe share a cigarette and a conversation
just some small talk and lies
about drop-dead, gorgeous dames in parisian cafés

and the indescribable joy of sweet tea

;

I am 23 years old;
I'm emotionally unstable;
financially bankrupt;
intellectually capable;
creatively brilliant;
I have a heart of gold;
I'm considering legally changing my name to *Scooter*;

I have plans to build a compound
     that will shame the Kennedys;
I might get something to eat tomorrow;
my dog is missing; in retrospect,
     it was probably a bad idea
     to name her *Traveler*

I don't follow sports;
the only time I dress up is
     when it's inappropriate to do so;
I count the change in my pocket,
     out of boredom and nervousness;
I am extremely fond of the semi-colon
     (my favorite punctuation);
     it expresses the true, rambling form that is me;

I am 23 years old;
I'm emotionally growing stronger;
financially augmenting stretching;
intellectually more than capable;
creatively brilliant;
I have a heart of gold;
I'm having second thoughts
     about the whole *Scooter* thing

untitled

I sat down to write about a kitten
Purring in gentle meekness
And in my mind, I saw only your figure
In all its alluring sleekness

I sat down to tell of the Orient
Of its masters of Tao and Zen
And in my mind, I saw only you
And you leaked forth from my pen

I sat down to paint a picture with words
Of a circus fair so gay
And in my mind, you were there
And you stole the scene away

morning

the sadistic rooster
pecks at my cerebellum
rousts me up and out
into the mad fields
where i dash about,
chasing tiny clovers
that slip through
my fingers

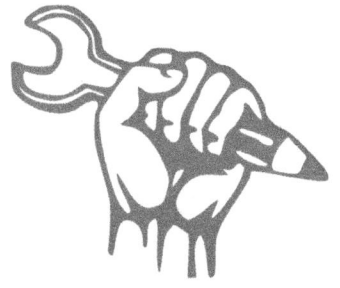

butcher, baker, poetry maker

some poems come slow

hard-won
biscuits
tedious sessions
of rolling pin
kneading out the lumps

mercilessly
cutting
punching
out
the
good
bits
with
cookie
cutter

pulling
something
recognizable
from the dough
unconscious
babble

slaughter the fatted calf
raw idea
trim away
fat
render the succulent cuts
into pan
grill to perfection,
someone's idea

some, you test
with a toothpick
for consistency

dangle the pan
faintly fanning
hinted aroma
a wave of your hand
in front of forums

allowing microphone
and crowd
to sniff them
tell
if they're done

deciding no,
toss them back
into oven
for a bit

even when you're "done,"
you somehow know...
it's still not...
quite...
right

pickle these preserves
on pantry shelf

keep the store
for the winter

some spring day,
emerge from cocoon
announcing the discovery
of last words

a far flung novel

miniseries conclusion
brings story together

long waits,
Tuesday to Tuesday
more tidbits of the tale

then,
entire seasons
of
waiting for
next season's
release

eventually,
full narrative
unfolds
itself
in the lap
and exhausted,
you say
no more

others
pop out
like children

already
perfect

a divine,
quiet voice
tickles your
insides

emphatic message

warning
of mother bear,
protection of cubs

touch not
one
precious hair
of this child's
sweet head

already
perfect

Birthday For John Michael

I'm crazy, you know
in the purest sense of the word

if ever there was such a thing
as sense, to be made of crazy

crazy because I bought a book of poetry
for my brother, who is not yet thirteen

I thought perhaps it might help
to stave off the impending madness of puberty
which will come at him with teeth bared

you see, there is madness in poetry
and therefore...
I am mad
for it

although I knew that a boy so young
would likely have no interest in such things
it seemed to me that he would be keenly interested
in his own tethering to sanity

a safety cable of reason
a single, tenuous thread
connection to the center
of the ever-revolving wheel

the coming of adulthood threatens to snip
with its callous, unfeeling scissor,
that scythe, insidiously harvesting
your voice
and your balls

I thought, just maybe
he'd be into feeling a little less crazy
for at least a few minutes,
here and there

such an incredibly crazy thought,
that a child would possess
such foresight

personally, I had found poetry
to be helpful in that department
to some slight degree

I thought perhaps
madness could somehow
cancel out
madness

nothing wrestles a man
from the grips
of time

nothing breaks
the bondage
cruel, chemical chaos
ripping through veins

growth spurts
voice changes
aching soreness
spurts of anger
undirected lust
new hunger
new hatreds

alas, I cannot save my beloved kin
from himself

he will
almost certainly
be every bit
as insane
as I was

as I am

crazy does not cease with puberty
it trucks on into old age
interspersed with other,
newer types of crazy

delusions of permanence
self-importance, purpose
relationships, jobs, families, friends
enemies, health, and illness
poverty and wealth
good and evil
truth and deception

mad stuff
all

every one of them
falsity, lies

bitter decoys
feinting us to the right
so that life can catch us
with the outside
hook
left
sex and death
do their perverse dances
on the tops of our skulls

each day,
we become men
crawling the slow trenches
of experience
climbing the umbilical maze
DNA ladders

maturity
illusions of manhood

ever disappearing horizon
carrot and stick

bell is sounded
sun pops its head up

test begins
eyes
spring open

it stops
when you
collapse
under
your own
weight

earth
scorched battlefield

long past
puberty
all the heated business
of adults
and their madnesses

struggles, overcome

having learned to kick the world
in its post-pubescent, adult balls
make it submit

new struggles appear
endless cycle
breeds like rabbits
and rats

pride in all
expect more

twist now, the land beneath you
twist the earth itself
into a better shape
stand over a kingdom

coax all
love and laughter
from bones of universe
seduce
make the worst jokes
laugh
crashing the party
enjoy

I lend you all good faith and hope
oh, my brother,
in your plight
of turning
into a man
I wish you well

and not crazy,
such as I

one day of each meaningless year,

we mark process
colorful balloon, frosting
pencil marks on the door frame

mere gesture
celebration
tragically comic

serial killer
steps out to get a pack of smokes
leaves us a note: *Back In Five*

compare and contrast
herculean task
survive
another year

absence of birthday ribbons
strangling
lead balloons
poison cake

hurts when no one...
brief moment that it takes

thanks for not dying...

better place,
with you

Car Trouble

What happened anyway?
Did the rubber band break?
What'll it cost, man?
Did the hamster escape?

Lemon discouragement
Ship, run aground
Circus clown car
Won't make a sound
Wheels no longer
Go round and round
Bummin' a way
Sure brings you down

The eagle has no wings

Once Battleship Wonder
Turned U-boat
Took a dive under
Wouldn't float
Perhaps I should invest in
A dog sled
Or a goat

What's that?
They're on sale?
I'll make a note

Rose Garden

The garden flaunts fresh petals
And so Martha defends her

Five county fair medals
Commemorate its splendor

Martha's arched and tired
Still so diligent in the use of her hours

The growing season always gets her fired
She's oh so alive amongst her flowers

> The simple ways
> The warmer days
> And how some
> Spent their spring

Clipping Smilax

so, I've been working
for this landscaping company
because I have this thing about eating:
I like to do it
every couple of days or so

and I have a money fetish
not to mention a guitar habit
to support, strings and stuff

so anyway, I've been working
for this landscaping company
throwing handfuls of chemical fertilizer
at bushes and shrubs and plants
hundreds of pounds of the stuff each day
and when I'm not doing that
I'm pulling weeds and
clipping smilax

so there I am,
walking around in these yards
that belong to immensely wealthy people,
thinking, "Wow! Man, If I had this!"

but I don't, and so
I get to hunt the elusive smilax beast

this creature only infests the flower beds
of rich folks in Landfall
and out on Figure Eight Island

you see, poor folks don't have smilax
they just have weeds
and the weeds just grow

and nobody cuts them
because nobody cares

they're too busy trying to control their electric bill
entirely too busy earning money for food
to worry about weeds

but these folks that play golf on Saturdays
and go sailing on Sundays
they're terrified of the stuff
and they pay me

wait...

I mean, they pay the landscaping company
to rid them of the problem

then, the landscaping company pays me
a relatively small fraction of that money

so there I am, just walking around
in the yards that belong to these
incredibly loaded people
and I come upon this shrub

of course, I immediately recognize it as a shrub
because, as a lawn care professional,
I have the requisite training to identify it as such;
since shrubbery is, after all,
my profession

and I notice it's got some smilax growing at its base
but I notice that this particular weed
is reaching the wrong way
that is, away from the bush
a savvy bit of smilax will always grow
into whatever it's close to

because that's what smilax does;
it requires water and nutrients from its host
and uses them to grow stronger

finally, it chokes out the host source that it's attached
itself to

which is, of course,
something that I simply cannot allow

since I get paid to
stop that from
happening

and it's nice to get paid
since I have this thing about food
and guitar strings

so, I go trudging around with the pruners
and I cut down the malicious bindweed at its base
since you can't pull the damn things up
because they have a bulbous root, like a sweet potato

weed killer just doesn't work
so you just keep cutting them back
every so often
hoping that eventually
they will get tired and give up their little fight
and die

so, here's this persistent little weed
wasting its time, going the wrong way
and bored as I am, despite how utterly fascinating
my work truly is
madman that I am, I start talking to it,
urging it to go the other way

I tell it that there are (maybe) thirty more seconds
before I whack it down to its weed death
and in my opinion, it should use this time
wisely

I assert my opinion that this would be best
accomplished
by turning and going the right way,
toward the source of its nutrition

or at very least, by making its peace
with the plant god

you know... whatever funerary type, last rites
might be proper for a weed, in its time of dying

then it occurs to me that so many of us are just
going the wrong way
and doing this so much of the time

I mean, we've got, what...
thirty more years?
thirty days?
thirty seconds?

before that great clipper in the sky
whacks us down to our deaths?

maybe that vine was rebelling
maybe it realized the pointlessness of its existence
maybe it decided to be different
just because it could

from time to time, I think of this little weed
being so close to the source of its nourishment
and yet choosing to go the other way
going where the action is not

and me, here in these immensely rich people's yards
pulling their weeds, clipping their fucking smilax
and going where (like this ostentatious little weed)
I will get a lot of dirt on me
and no satisfaction

no mental, physical or spiritual satisfaction
and I am now seriously questioning my choices

we are all so very often
just biding time

me, I'm working
for this landscaping company
because it beats
flipping burgers
and digging ditches;
I speak from firsthand experience
on both counts

it staves off the bill collectors
and it buys guitar strings
(at least two or three)

and when I get caught up
I'll quit...
seek my true path for awhile

until I need to get a job again...
flipping burgers,
digging goddamned ditches
or clipping smilax

untitled

my coffee table is immortal

you, on the other hand,
barely amusing

energy, matter
never destroyed

take on new forms

neither
ever
never
done

anything real,
of consequence

amusing to somebody
impossible

all creation
end
in and of itself
end
of itself

masterful production
theater

play
the part
well played

long play

if it sounds as though it was recorded in a closet
if it's scratchy and coarse

if it moans about a woman, the woe that she unwound
if it sobs of how it

   "ain't never loved a man... the way that..."

if it tells of howling winds that wailed
as he wept and bled red blood on the tracks
at dawn, stone drunk, eyes burning from no sleep

if it's old, weathered, hard to find
its cover is worn, torn at the edges
if it asks even the willow to weep

if you have to twirl it around to make it dance
stick a needle into it to get it juiced up and
make it *talk*

then it's for me

put it on my plate with biscuits and gravy,
some *salt peanuts*
and a glass of iced tea or whiskey
just a little *spoonful* to wash it down

all you spirits, invisible
hiding in black, haunted items
of seemingly ordinary,
lifeless matter tucked into closets,
stacked away in garages
and on lonely bookshelves

in *the midnight hour*, you wake,
and i hear your phantasms
rollin' and tumblin' lonely voices, crying out...

    "i can't be satisfied."

histories, written in jagged tourmaline
the souls of the long-dead wander my hallways
because there, the acoustics are better;
the ghost can hear itself asking

    "when will i be loved?"

hearing ourselves speak, we may know we are still real

my honored guests,
let me help you all out of your jackets
and into my eager ear

warm my tired bones with the fierce, hot glow
of your glass, hellfire tubes

whisper to me your secret prayers
shout at me in your hoarse, staticky voices

let me know your wicked, gooseflesh ecstasy
awaken me to the siren call of your legion devils
speaking into my soul, possessing me

work your roots and tricks;
all that unholy hoodoo, heaping brimstone

pour your midnight *white lightning* into me
with two slumbering snake fangs
certain death, popping right out of the walls
and pulsing through your thin veins
into my frail, unprepared heart

your dim whorehouse lights shining in darkness
illuminating my room through the screen doors
of your temple, constructed of wood and chrome
tweed and blood

tell your hidden priests of the back alleys
swamps and big cities and prisons
to recite their unholy incantations

open those dusty, secret scrolls to me
dripping the black wax of their dark spells
onto my paralyzed being, unable to move
slack jaw rapture as you speak in tongues

entranced by the winding serpent
its thin, diamond tongue, full of sin
following that endless, circular pathway
of ruin and heartbreak
down to the center of your bullseye core
where only emptiness waits

    "when the music's over...
    turn out the lights."

open to me, your doubly dark books
forbidden, black tablets
open only to *me and the devil*
teaching me a muddy, ghetto knowledge
of flesh, *love in vain*, horrible accidents,
fortune, failure, jealous rage, and
murder in the red barn

quiet my spirit with your surreal, sublime
white noise hiss, posing the essential question...

    "who do you love?"

the serpent opens its hungry, hinged jaw
stretching forth its flickering, needlelike tongue
to taste that forbidden, onyx knowledge
lapping it up from your obsidian offering plate

i want to feel the rhythmic pulse
of your vibrating, paper lips
and your round, heavy
magnetic heart

release into me, the wild madness
of your invocations
inciting pagan dancing,
making you *shake your moneymaker*

tormented bursts of spontaneous weeping
and the sweet, sunday splendors
of a million miles of cathedral organ pipe

tell me all your stories
burst me open...

too long have i been
closed off by silence

i want to know all
of your forgotten mysteries

kindly introduce me
to all your dead

and your soon
to be dying

jack-in-the-box

I have just finished reading
The Last Night of the Earth Poems
by Charles Bukowski

and this will probably reek of it
but that is perfectly ok with me

paying homage to other writers is good
and while I will not attempt it intentionally...

flattery
is the highest form
of imitation
or something like that

I mention all this in forward

the point is, Bukowski said
he despaired at writers who would
ask him for advice
commentary, criticism
and worst of all,
collaborations

they didn't understand
that you have to
just sit down
and bang it out

he said they don't want to write

they want to
succeed
at writing

I agree

it should be evident that if you're making art
—and not just a paycheck—
then you should only write from a place of
passionate desire

you don't try to wind up the muse
like some goddamn jack-in-the-box

you can't meet her at a poetry seminar
you don't pick her up in a bar

still, my father
would plead with me to
get a real job

and I would
pleaded with him
(to no avail)
that I was

already working

that is until I finally got the good sense
to cut my family
completely out of my life

I write;
I was written into the script of the world
to play the part of a writer

I play music
this jack-in-the-box
was wound-up
to play music

of course,
I also drink
and so I am
drunk
for drinking

many people
(*real people*, mind you;
not those impostors you see
out on the sidewalks)
have genuine talent

but only a few of them
have the guts
to shove it
down the throat
of the public

until the public agrees that it's good

anymore, it's just not enough to be *good*
or even *great*, for that matter

you have to be *popular* and *profitable*
or else they don't think it's art

this says far more about people
than it does about good art
but that matters about as much as...
never mind

brute force,
this is the only course of action for success
in this cesspool of tiny-minded little shits
who listen with other people's ears
and see with other people's eyes

unfortunately, the untalented schmucks
often understand it, while some of the greatest
geniuses do not

we wouldn't even know who Emily Dickinson is
except that someone found her poetry after her death
and they had the good sense to publish it

she submitted a scant few pieces and some
shit head, hack editor
(who probably never wrote a decent letter,
much less a good poem)
raked her over the coals...

she never really got over it;
kept it all to herself,
from there on out

thankfully, many good artists do stick it out
but dear god, so do the bad ones

I have no patience for dribble
especially when I have
distilled the bile, myself

I often find such an intolerance
for my shortness of brilliance
that it is a wonder I work at all
but I hammer away,
chiseling tasteless
bits of cliché
say what I must say
drink until I play
type until the day
death will come
to haul me away

maybe there is a god
of smiling at trifle inconsistencies

loves us
in spite of ourselves

probably a stretch

but I know quite well
the god of
fuck you

I pray at the Holy Altar of His divine strength
for the conviction and fortitude
necessary to War with one's haters

those who hate you merely because you took the
desperate stab at the guts of life
the one that they were entirely too afraid to take

this gracious God shares with me
the Gospel of Out

get out of my way
get out of my life
get out of my head
get out of my dreams

when you have come here,
only to dump your stinking,
haughty, disdainful
loaf of disapproval,
right on top of all my hard work,
then verily I sayeth unto thee,
by the decree of the Most High

fuck off

all the way off

I believe in me

In fact, I believe in me
enough for the both of us

    and therefore,
    your presence
    is no longer
    required

       I craft my own realities now

         and my supervisor
          gives me less
              shit
           than yours
             gives you

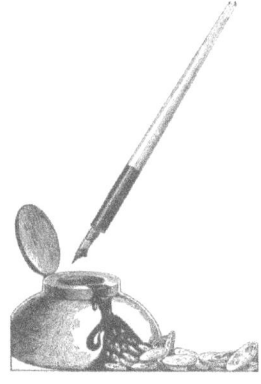

         less than you
           gave me

         anyway...
         yes, dad,

           I already
            have
              a fucking
                 job

persistence

no one
listens,
anymore

a lie

no one
ever did
listen

enter the arena
egalitarian terms
well understood

pick up the serpent
see if it strikes

curtains quickly closing
on darkness

curtains closing slowly
over centuries

master the serpent
consume hero

become an invisible
tornado of nightmares
unstoppable force

a public bludgeoning
of dull-witted sheep
crack over and into the denseness
of skulls, both brutal and boorish

all their simple eggs
cracked out of those simpleton brainpans
and melting into your
golden frying pan

a never sleeping silence
allowing the free moment
to pass, unhindered
smooth and calm

beat them all
into submission
make them all
eventually
nod,
applaud

feed them what you would have them eat

until they forget all previous
stale staples of what is
not yours

championing the cause of
all that is

write the histories of victors
and hard-won spoils
of desperate war

Saint Machiavelli
smiles upon your
holy endeavor

fabulous

i can sit

                              here

all night

slunk down
into a
naked
cigarette

staring

at

        dairy

                crates

my

        chic,

                stolen

                        furniture

it's a bit forced, isn't it?

the last lines of the poem
are deliberately curt
the sloppiness of it,
how it abruptly ends
in that uncouth
and haphazard way

distorted reflections
of well-rehearsed hurt
terminating in a dowdy hissy fit
feigning amends
the fakery of youth
a disgraceful display

the words must be slurped
from a child's sippy cup,
to give full and accurate depiction;
its finish can't be easy
it mustn't be orderly or adult
its manner must forego any style

absent any pseudo-explanations
rationalizations to quit and give up
well, it just isn't your fiction;
the reader must be left queasy,
choking, as i did, on insult

contending with that overwhelming, wrathful urge
the one which so politely invites me to
rip that saccharine, serpentine smile
right off your pretentious face

pocket change

narrated by a silly cartoon moose

eighty-four single cents
are my pocket's occupants

they are small cents, you see
but still
they fill
my pocket
to its
capacity

you see,
my pocket
has grown
smaller

while my debt
has grown
taller

and while my
workload
grows taller
and taller

i continue to
get smaller
and smaller

for the love
of a dollar

untitled

I'm gonna make a movie
Starring you,
About me

I'm gonna make a million
Cold, hard currency

I'm gonna make it happen;
Just you wait and see

I'm gonna make a plan...
When it comes to me

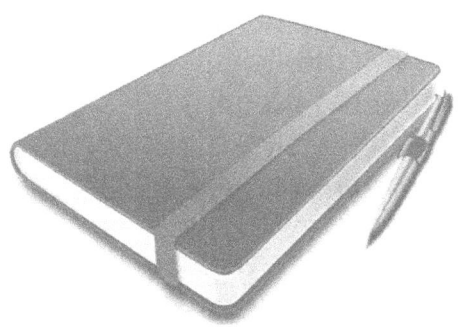

rain on paper

rain on paper
words clouded
life of language written
riddled with tears

in the grip of an immoveable sadness
projection of an erroneous path
walking in the footsteps of failure

how can these things be casually pushed aside?

"it's just that demon life has got you in its sway."

at least, that's what mick jagger tells me

nice guy;
sings to me from the tiny speaker
in the dashboard of my father's pickup truck

dad is scouring the local chain bookstores
looking for books
about computer programs and software

seeking synthesis;
a computable measure of productivity
maximization of enjoyment
transient wonders of technology
available to the fingertips of modern men
cruise the information superhighway

i play guitar and write more poetry;
poetry about wanting more understanding
peace of mind and music

i write about how music lovingly kneads my head,
like a talented masseuse,
working knuckles along tense lines;
rubbing out the kinks

a master pizza maker,
tossing the supple dough
until it's just right

music, collections of sound waves
sound waves are just air and vibrations
slapping against your head

there's a great deal of sweet music
in things like courage and willpower

the willingness to cut through
hum-drum, everyday horror

things that no one has taught me,
things that i am learning
all on my own

weariness can easily overtake you
on rainy afternoons like today
when everything seems
very wrong

when you are so incredibly certain
that you are not of this place

not of these people
not of this time

dad offers to buy me a book
so i pick out a book on taoism

he stares at it the way an aboriginal woman
might stare at a cappuccino maker

asks me, "you sure that's what you want?"

little omens such as this
sometimes affirm for us
that our path,
while dark,
is somehow
correct

returning home, i pop in a tori amos cd,
and she warns

> *"can't stop what's coming.*
> *can't stop what is on its way."*

a retreat is just as valid
a tactical maneuver
as an attack

it's not always enough
to take the hill,
to conquer new ground

sometimes you must
burn the bridges
so that the enemy
may not pursue you

sometimes, you simply must
burn every last bridge
to the past

Once

I once saw a masterpiece
That was left undone

I once met a liar
Who had no tongue

I once played a game
That could not be won

But there's still so much
Left to do

I once met a man
With no color in his face

I once kissed a woman
Whose lips had no taste

And as for the new world,
I've been all over that place

But I've yet to meet another
Like you

untitled

the morning
is a bad time for magic

back from the brink of madness
tragic, cold, wandering exile
tarnished and rusty

inches of cosmic dust
on the boots

orbiting earth
fetal position
without all questions

a green apple
borrowed
is not a red one
returned

chess-like military moves
crystallization of opinions
clenching teeth
pale ape knuckles
buckets of cliché
sickness

sorry for
mentioning;
at other times
don't care

divide time
in picking up
the floor

knocked
down

hurling rocks
at the sun

trying to kill
realization

and still,
the morning

offers
no
magic

untitled

i have a collection of
painfully obvious statements
that i keep on display
in the den

they're only for
special occasions

entertaining guests

now, it seems
one of them has
gone missing

you wouldn't, by any chance,
happened to have seen it,
would you?

no, i only ask
because...

it's just that...

well, i overheard you
talking to your friend,
and well...

oh, never mind

i'm sure it'll
pop up

somewhere

prodigy

I wish   I was more of a musician
I may   need to practice more

I wish   I was a virtuoso
I might   even settle for being less of a poet

    probably not.

I am too tired to play my guitar
Not that I have done anything tiring;
Just tired

I've been working hard at not working

drinking and smoking is an easy job
but hey, someone has to do it

it truly is an easy job;
it's just that
nothing else is easy
I feel too damned old
to be this young

Burroughs said, *"The problem with poets
is that they go from adolescence to old age
with nothing in between."*

I hate when people speak such plain truth;
it only clouds the real issue,
which is that I'm almost out of beer

after all, why torture the poor truth?
making it grovel and crawl on its belly
over the muddy earth of this world

have some sympathy for the truth
what with the modern circumstances
it must contend with

set the truth free;
it would do the same for you

set it free from all of your
tired grasping at its throat

what's that old saying?

if you love something,
kill it and put it out of its misery

if it comes back to life...
well, it probably still isn't worth the effort

or something like that... I forget the particulars

the problem is, I tell myself
too many truths
with just enough lies thrown in
to cloud it all

we begin to lose track of what's what

I want to play music
but I despise playing by myself
it's a kind of musical masturbation

and even masturbation
seems boring lately

worse still,
playing music by yourself
with no audience

that's like masturbating
with no pornography
to inspire you,
get you over the edge

music, like good sex,
makes it all better

there is no doubt
that these days
I am in doubt
about
how to keep
my demons
on a short leash

if I am to survive
and pursue this lust
for poetry and music

however,
I am quite sure
that I will find
some suitable excuse
for binding them

after all...
excuses are my *forte*

shackle them,
just long enough
to put them all
to work

maybe I'll build an empire

untitled

we find gratitude
in the little strengths
which we build in these teensy hours
between forethought
and our commitment
to various pressing activities

each moment dies
its little death

if we fail in the essential
recognition of this

we trip over
cumbersome
blind
lack of grace

jest and naiveté
have their charm and place

but can we entirely subsist
on such a meager staple?

need something thicker
something that fills the swollen belly
in the hot stench of summer

a query sent by a neuron, moron messenger
the filling of an order, essential
requisitioned supplies

summit of flesh
bubbling
ideas

grant us more of this,
the quiet existence

easy death
still-going moments

fish shot with rubber band guns
in size-less ponds

give me simpleton child smiles

the play of light
and the turning of bright,
pointless, children's toys

can the sagacity of these proceedings
be rightly questioned?

I shall then play
closer to the boundaries
color for a bit, inside the lines

for now, kick the particle blind eyes
into darkness

your box of sand
or mine

I will
ease myself
along

wind up toy

if it is
conceivable

they are
doing it

anything
can be
done

in here

small

in the reflection
is you

and you,
looking into the
reflection

and the reflection
of the reflection
of the reflection
of the reflection
is me

but it is
only
you

all those
so very many things
that say
so awful much
about you

so much so,
that there is
no room left
for anything else;

even
you

Clarity

I was a house one day
And I watched them
All-day

Watched them go about their lives
Watched them
When they beat their wives
And they scarred the baby

And I could not help him
Oh, I could not help him

It's not for me to say
Who's right or wrong
In the world today
In opinions

But I know one thing

To hurt someone is wrong
To hurt someone is wrong

This, I see clearly
And there is no doubt in me

Yes, this
I see clearly

To Jazz

One flew into the cuckoo's nest
    heroes were fitted for padded, white linen
       medicated bed sheets

And lovers were tossed
    to the silent scream of the streets

No one, mi boy
    expects it when their heroes die

But carry on with a thoughtful sigh

Remember the good times,
    the beach circle signs

Stay out of the dark
    it rips you to shreds

Who harkens not the warning
    cuts the threads

It need not take you,
    oh, beautiful brother of pristine light

I raise a toast
    to your success and might

Here's to you,
    cashing in each breath

Knocking the teeth
    out of the jaws of death

pick me up something sweet

sometimes i am too far...
far tooo intoxicated
to fly this bird

far too intoxicated
to be operating a sophisticated
and potentially dangerous
piece of machinery

such as this

i am completely aware
of the fact that i am only
partially aware
of everything

i am only partially aware
of the fact that i am
completely aware
of everything

some people are too, far...
tuu sober
to think soberly

they never sit next to themselves
never cheat off of their own rolling papers

they never eavesdrop on their own private
conversations
they never howl at the walls
or bay at frogs or croak at the moon
they never talk to the trash can like i do

but somebody needs to
put that fucker
in its goddamned place

it keeps eating up all my poetry

they never loosen the cogs
or grease the wheel
that wasn't squeaky anyway
after all, you can go mad
acting sane all the time

you can't pretend forever;
at some point, you have to
let down the facade
blow off some pressure
clean out the pipes

i've no idea how you people hold up
those heavy masks
for such interminable periods

what with the payment being due on the bmw
saving up for the kid's education
and coping with all the inconvenient fallout
from the death of what little love
was left in your little black, withering hearts

it seems like you'd get tired, bored
need to put them down for a little while;
at least long enough to run out
to get something from the store

but hey, if you *are* going to the store...

Preacher

I.

Lay it on thick
As much as you can muster
But remember
As you lay those yellow,
Bilious bricks, brother
That the truth
Shall set you free

You may find that freedom
Is not all that it's
Cracked up to be
Released from the protection
Of all those sheltering lies
No safe harbor
Nowhere to hide

Exposed, even to yourself
Naked before the Lord

II.

Woe to the preacher
Who heeds not
His own advice
This is I
The victim
Of my own device

Summon sister wisdom
Brother pride
Denies her
But brand yourself a fool
You may only grow
The wiser

minimum wage

"who do i think i am?"
you ask

why,
i am joe schmoe,
don'tcha know?

i am he who plays
by the rules
the servant of fools

i am the scrounger
of pocket change

i am he
who will exchange
himself
for gain

you know my name

yours is the same

I need

I'd give anything
    for nothing in particular;
        something worth hiding,
            someone for sliding...
                    into

I need
    a woman's hand,
        tangled in my hair
            softly crying,

                "give me more."

I need
    a hundred thousand voices,
        strangling the tube-amplified air
            screaming,

                "give me more."

I need
    naked eyes,
        dangling in a reading stare
            thinking,

                "give me more."

untitled

these fruits fall
at the feet of lucky men

to see friends
with their eyes

taste with them
the tastes of things
which are not sweet
but necessary

watching them swallow
five-pound pills of pain

seeing them choke
on sorrowful sounds

sounds born of the harsh nature of this existence

all things that you would not
sprinkle on your food
by choice

unselfishly stomached

the memory of kin
boils tears
over the edge of every pot

weeping is merely
being alive;
nothing more
to be said of it

at certain times it is
inappropriate
to comment

as with a strong men
who is your friend
who has lost a brother

death slips
into the gallery

nothing replaces
priceless treasures

something
substitutes

the inability
to explain any of this
bothers all
who attempt it

and so, we never speak of it

and still, no one escapes it
one places oneself firm
in that place, in that time

there is no recourse,
only the telling of pain

you sit and gnaw
upon the sour fruit
of heartache
not for the taste
and not for the sustenance

since there is none there
to be had

but for the solace
for the strong man,
who is your friend,
who has lost a brother

who has offered you
a place at his table,
while he is weak and weeping
and would turn any other man
away

you sit with him,
sipping politely
at the cup
of loss

you drink your fill
and ask if
perhaps,
he might be so kind
as to let you have
some of his

a question which
would be rude
under any other circumstances

but of course,
he cannot share it

his cup will remain full
until his eyes drain thoroughly
his heart, wholly emptied

the fruits on his plate are his alone

but your presence sweetens his lot
just a bit

assures him that he does not have to
eat alone

you distract him,
so that he does not notice
each, individual
falling hour

we find fruits
lying on the ground
still edible
semi-sweet

we gain strength
and good, sweet hope

and here, these fruits fall

offering their
strange compensation

a bit of the nectar
of memories

sweet
and otherwise

it's a lovely piece, miss

I.

so much longer now
from that time
still possessed
by the immanence of jazz
covered by the template of Orion
knitted neatly into
the socks of lesser euphoria
the tides rise
plumes of smoke, as well
and a distant, ambivalent buzz
in the eyes of those who
sleep too late into the day
who rise on eagle feathers
in the dawn of the soul's quietness

being bright and quiet,
there, a peace ascends
on the vehicle of not needing
and instead, doing
and the excitement of knowing
that death is coming soon
and being prepared for it and fearless of it
refusing to become ensnared
by the mad smirks of ghosts yet to come;
to tame them and make them wait

II.

careful where you sleep, brother, and when
I'd like to see you cultivate
a fcw acrcs of this jungle
before you dash off to
join the nether folk
I'd like to see the plans
for that castle of yours
come into fruition

III.

It's a lovely piece of poetry
you've got there, miss

may the peace of the morning
place itself into your restless spirit
bridle, harness it
and brush your long, lush hair
free of the dark night
and its stinging flies
you are the pretty pony
of my tomorrow's hoping
fill your pale, smooth belly
with the oats of a
satiating enlightenment
and the seed of a thousand stars

feel the unceasing caresses
of endless jazz chords
brushing through the fibers of slanted time
clearing new ground
sounding the arrival
of your entity
with horns of infinite madness
forgiven

IV.

these pages will be
blown away by May winds

I hope only that
you heard

if for no other
reason...

that you might
remember

my voice

Beef Jerky

Straps
Saddles
Leather
Salty breath
Rough riders
Ride rough rides
To frontier deaths
This, to be a man
Quest
For fire
Freedom
The good fight
Women and whiskey
Powder and ball
Barrels alight
Law of the land
Brutal
Western blacksmith
Forge a boy
Into a man

We are the riders of the weary.
What shall we say of women and whiskey?

reverie

a pleasance
abounding

a garden of sound
grape, morning glory,
bougainvillea, moonflower,
jasmine, honeysuckle
and trumpet vine,
climbing their
lattice way
to heavens of rapture

mint, rose, marjoram
and lavender
creeping ever forward
overtaking mind
overgrown with
luxury

surmounting
details
of contractual
inconvenience

waves of
par excellence
ascending into
fevered pitch

corkscrewed
into
naked ears
this,
the music

that I have yet
to play

the dream
I must
live-out
beyond
my sleep

the magic
that I must
coax out of
the possession
of studious devils

the mystery
I must pry
from the tight hands
of prick tease gods

music
more divine
than all else

pristine as the
flame
that devoured
Jerusalem

Aptitude Testing

my realms of
experience
are

music
manual labor
magick
poetry
madness

madness doesn't
pay very well
and unless you are
a famous artist;
no one takes the insane seriously anymore...

damn shame

it seems to have fallen
out of style

poetry doesn't pay
much better
but the hours
are far more flexible
and it's often rather useful
for picking up women

music has lots of potential for huge profits
but it requires great effort, practice,
and real determination
and somebody influential
who can pull strings
while you pluck them

the drugs and the girls are
definitely of a
much higher quality
than those available to
poets and madmen

magick makes
everything better
and obviously,
by better, I mean...
stranger

yet, it doesn't sit well
on most letterhead
or on any resume

which is odd
and angled,
any way you slice it

you'd think
that any company
would be
more than glad
to snatch up a guy
who can make some
peculiar shit happen
in a pinch

but the groupies
are a mixed bag
of hotties and has;
some suck your cock
and others,
only your
bloody soul

of course,
there's always
washing dishes
and digging ditches
for these,
there are no groupies
no drugs
fall from the sky

but injuries
regularly
jump up
from the
ground

bouncing Betty
part and parcel
stock and trade

the pay is
absurd
and the benefits?
well,
you get to be
insulted by idiots
on a daily basis

and the decidedly
negative implications
of these last facts

place you right back
in the job description
of the madman

untitled

i am a drop
in the proverbial bucket

when set aside,
compared to

legends
heroes of
yesterday

thousands of pages
i have so few

i will write more
i promise

i feel ashamed

i am apologizing to you,
all of you

for not being...
more

but i will
work
harder

create
something

beautiful

untitled

Shelter?

> Many make do with a park bench
> A canvas tent will keep you out of the weather
> The world still possesses a few good, kind folk
> Who'll take you in

Food?

> The trees have fruits and berries
> The fields will yield a harvest
> The Earth is a proponent of beasts
> The waters have fish

Clothes?

> These you can fashion, improvise

Shoes?

> Only in winter

Cars?

> Your feet can carry you fine
> A horse can take you farther

Money?

> Honest work brings an honest wage
> Love of money is folly for fools
> Better to fill your head and soul
> Than your wallet

Friends?

> Those who accompany you
> During times of poverty and misfortune
> Those who uplift you and
> Lead you in positive directions
> You need no others

Possessions?

> These are warm, spring winds
> Ever-fleeting joys

Work?

> Builds character, strength of mind and body
> Garbage men are equal to congressmen

Family?

> Those who love the true you
> These are your family
> The real trick is not
> Discovering who your true family is
> But who the true you is

Strife, Anger, Apathy, Regret, Worry?

> What for?
> No time

Dreamers, Lovers?

> Very good things indeed

sad haiku

two lovely women
too bad that neither is mine
they are on their own

seasoned grease blues

I'm gonna take myself
a handful of pills
and lay down on my deathbed

Lord, I said I'm gonna take myself
a handful of pills
and drop on down, dead

Because if you don't come on back to me, baby
you know I'm bound to lose my head

I ain't never before felt so sad
oh mercy, you know I feel so blue

Ain't never before been so awful sad
ain't never before been so terrible blue

I'll turn up in the river, darlin'
kissin' fishes and
clutchin' a soggy picture of you

two choruses, no more

I have more to offer
than you or I will ever know

so you... myself...
my dearest and closest me

would do well to remember this
to partake of the wine of faith in you

hearken now, dear reader
that this wine is untainted and is indeed fit
to be drunk by any passerby

the natives will grow restless from time to time
and the palace will have new sentries
the old ones having been executed for treason

the court jesters will be killed off
for not being funny
they will be summarily replaced

but you will remain the same
and you will continue

little do you know,
my uncertain friend
that you will rise, all too soon
to present the world with a feat, most superb

the realm of fiasco has been safely navigated
in advance
and you will perturb the ear of failure
with your modern rendition of the champion's dance

you will take Charlie's advice
and keep it brief

> *"blow anything more than two choruses*
> *and baby, you're just practicing."*

the circus continues
and the spotlight falls on you
soon enough

you will perform all those stupid pet tricks
with a marvelous abandon

knowing full well that
all art and good taste
is nothing but stupid pet tricks
when boiled down to their purest,
most authentic form

and you will delight in this perverse knowledge

all of that stupid pressure
suddenly off and away
turning into something
that you happily
forgot

nothing,
my good friend
is left

nothing
but joy

great things

sometimes we do great things
merely to justify all of the
stupid and selfish things

trust bleeds
true red blossoms

connections to the past
encampments of fearful friends
dead tomorrows

we sing

torture is a commodity
in the sense that
you can measure it,
even trade it for goods
or other services

in a kind of sense
that is unfit
to be called
sense

clever devices you may devise
clover rises, and then it dies

I have stupidities to give you
in the clever disguise
of things which you desire

I never meant to deal in lies...
it just sort of happened that way

there is a trendy line of thinking
that paints everything in tangerine shades
of coincidental bus station buttons

we do well to worship this absurdity
in all of its serene forgiving forgetfulness

piano blues are beautiful
beautiful enough to fit in
anywhere

a perfect ruse to distract you
from the fact that I have nothing
groundbreaking to offer you here
my being excused
occurs in light of the fact that
you needed nothing,
and nothing...
I have faithfully delivered

clever devices you may devise
clover rises, and then it dies

modern rationale is just as good a place to hide
as the old schools of thought
all dried and purified
coated in the honey of forgetfulness

one of your own
is trying to poison you

comical, lethal, all our aimless
stabbing away our eyes
with fierce and practical reasoning;
it is wise to be aware of this

reboot the system

After Taxes

I awoke one dismal payday morn
Knowing that it was time
To go out and sweat in the sun
So I could collect my two and a quarter and a dime

When I realized this measly portion
Was already more or less spent
Some one-sixty of it was set aside
To pay the week's portion of the rent

Of course, I'd have to have
Some ten bucks or so for gas
So car would move to job
Where I would bust my ass

Saturday and Sunday are mine
Monday through Friday, I'm more than beat
So when I get home, I'll need some
Fifty dollars worth of food to eat

When I crawl into bed each evening,
I feel sore and stiff and hardly half alive
Now, what kind of recreation and relaxation
Can I buy for the remaining five?

punch clock

60, 70 hours

50 weeks

they rarely speak
if ever
at all

lack of sleep
stares

bludgeoning holes
in a lifetime

swing shift syndrome

hammer and anvil blues

the schedule
allows no time
for depression

the benefits
do not cover
dental, divorce,
eyecare, suicide

stop hovering
around the water cooler

no one is
watching

On The Way Back

onthewayback
thingsruntogether
and get clouded and

                    obskuured

pyur intention seeeems forrrced
appears as perversion

hell seeing heaven
other side of the door
nothing but pain

seeeems
anything you do
looks fayk
misanterpreded

call yerself
a phony

continue

force of habit
conviction
stubernnnesss

unwillingness to change
ugly status quo
chickn
in evry pot
the only onthewayback
there is

untitled

genius
comes

eccentric

quiet

creeping
discouragement

paranoia

sets
in

loose,
sinking
stone

wreaks
havoc

this book

this book is not mine
my girl checked it out of the library for me
thought I'd like it

I do

I renewed it once, already
it's a substantial size; I haven't finished it yet
collected works of a famous poet

this writer has an excellent range
simultaneously capable of
great optimism;
also abysmal pessimism

hatred, fear, hope, and love
and other, delightful,
made up things

but mostly just dark
and ugly things

this book goes places with me
I read it on the toilet, at my desk
in the red chair, the one that is too short for me
but is the perfect size for her
on the couch
waiting in the van
sitting in bed

this book comforts me
even though this writer
is dark and punched full of rough,
bloody holes

ridden with the diseased potholes
of a destroyed life;
gutted like a fish,
still wriggling
in defiance

this book
makes me smile
makes me hurt

makes me laugh until pain cuts through my stomach
and it becomes challenging to breathe

it has made me cry
at least once

I think the author of this book
would either smile or sneer at that
depending on the day
his mood at the time

I find this book lying around
on my desk, the bathroom floor
the bed, the couch
wherever

you could say that the author
has gotten around, right?

hardy fuckin' har har

and that's the thing
about this book

it goes from the majestic to the terrible, the profane
jumps from the sublime to the sadistic, masochistic
and just plain ol' dirty

I love it

it matches me perfectly
this book suits my style

it has a shitty front cover

which is a nice picture of the author

and that would be fine
except that the author is not at all attractive

and even if he was,
the publisher covered it with an opaque dust jacket
that I suppose they thought looked chic
when in fact, it's just plain bullshit
it looks ridiculous

but I think the author would have appreciated being
covered up
not so easily

seen

a kind of anonymity,
however thin and half-hearted the effort
he'd say that even this
weak smokescreen
was welcome

bullshit dust cover?
better than nothing;
naked

damn thing is torn anyway
makes it look like it's been
to California and back

I think that is where the author lived
Hell, California
that's near L.A., isn't it?
it doesn't say in the book
or else I haven't gotten that far yet

I read this book slowly,
a few pages at a time
a slow, laborious descent
into whatever special kind of hell
this strange landscape is
the mind of this mad person

the only signals draped in fog
the only map being
bad dust jacket despair

I don't have any particularly clever
or snappy way of
wrapping this up

but that fits fine with the theme
you may safely say the author's world is
somewhat nihilistic,
full of comic and frequently painful
loose ends

so, there
now you have
my book report

untitled

she said I was
wasted

that I was something like pearls,
cast to swine

an unseen painting, an unheard poem

I don't have time to
express my feelings
about any of that

because I have to get up early for work
and I need my sleep

I comfort myself with the notion
that I can be a diamond later
in some distant...
tomorrow

in that (much later) time
I will pound the victory drum
that summons
paradise

on a weekend,
when I am rested up
and feeling a little more
optimistic
about existence

meanwhile,
I'll build
other people's castles

I am a builder of
other people's dreams

I can no longer
afford my own

she was all I had
then, she skipped the program, too

so now, I am penniless and perverse
penitent and prolific
parched and profane

and she has the nerve to ask me

> *when will you shape the mist of vision*
> *and solidify the sound of union?*

but I heard none of that asinine question
because I was out the door
in my car and halfway home
before I ever even
left the room

electric messages of sleep
are now popping across
my synapses
neural networks
nodding out
I am head over heels in love
with the notion of sleep

tomorrow is payday

it's best to focus
on that

I can spare some magic for my loftier aspirations
after I've paid the electric bill

and I'll think about her...
after I'm good and drunk

one day, I'll look back
and happily remark
that most of my dreams
have come true

at least the important ones

of course,
she won't be there
to share them

and somehow...
that...

seems to be
the one part
of all of it

that makes me think
that just maybe...

there is somebody
up there...

somebody

looking out
for me

Ben's Word

Ben made up a word
He was very proud of the fact that he had created
His very own word
After all, not everyone has their own special word
Actually, only a very few people do
Since most folks find that they get along just fine,
With the ones that are already available

It was a long, somewhat hard to pronounce word
Its meaning was tied to not one but several different
Equally obscure concepts regarding things
Most people had little to no frame of reference for

Nevertheless, it was Ben's word, and he just adored it
Thought it was really neat

Of course, he used it all the time to make sure that
People were familiar with it

Of course, no one had the slightest clue just
What the devil he was talking about

And because of this, everyone felt awkward when
He would invariably halt the flow
Of an otherwise nicely progressing conversation
To explain the rather difficult meaning of his word
A word that caused the people who heard it
(And a great many people did have to endure it)
To reach down into their forgotten vocabularies
And dust off one that they did understand
One that they hadn't used since college
That word being *superfluous*

But being of good, solid breeding and etiquette
These people would bite their tongues and smile

Only the engineers in the crowd
Showed any interest at all in learning what it meant
Everyone else went all slack-jawed and silent
And honestly, nobody cared
What the engineers thought, anyway
Ben only had a chance to drop it on them
Because nobody else would talk to them at parties

He tried in vain to convince people to use his word
That is, to enter it into the common vernacular

Despite his protests and all his arguments
As to why everyone should have it in their vocabulary
It was a painfully obvious fact that *no one cared much*
For Ben's word

Everyone, down to the last man, woman, child,
Dog, cat, and goldfish just *dismissed it*, outright

They did this as politely as possible
But found that Ben's persistence in the matter was
Shall we say, a bit taxing?
They found that,
If they were to remain courteous and civil,
They must find some way to disengage
From the conversation and... *walk away*

Ben wrote endless letters
To all the publishers of dictionaries
And not just the well-known ones, either; *all of them*
His letters were all very formal, very passionate
Each one firmly asserted that his new word
(Which wasn't very new at all by this late date)
Was becoming a hot new item in the global lexicon
And he assured them that its exclusion
Would most certainly bring ridicule upon their heads

But after many, many years and many, many letters
There were still no takers

None of the thesauruses would include it
They asserted that they had
More than enough words already
Ben was hurt by this
But covered it up by scoffing

> "You'd think that if they were so smart and had so many
> words, they'd find a better way to say it! Something a
> little better than 'We have more than enough words,
> already!'"

The last part was always a fair amount higher in pitch
And laced with a distinct bitterness
One that grew more piercing
With each subsequent retelling
And there were a *great many* retellings

So, Ben moped and pouted for a long while
He was often seen mumbling to himself
Sometimes, he went down the street
In the middle of the night
Doing strange things, like
Shouting his word up at a window
Until someone would throw a shoe at him
Or a lamp or a large, decorative, scented candle
Or whatever was close;
Once the rage became too much for them

A cycle ensued, a most disturbing cycle
Of waking up the neighborhood, getting arrested
The charges were usually disturbing the peace
Being released without bail
The Sheriff and Ben's mother were... *special friends*

Staying quiet for a few weeks
Then doing it all over again

After the fifth time that he was
Locked up for public nuisance
They put Ben in the nuthouse for a short stay
There, he received counseling and medication

He made it very clear that he'd
Seen the error of his ways
He intended to get better
He wrote fervent promises of how he would
Turn himself into a productive member of society

But once they released him, he began again
That very same night, in fact

The entire time, he'd only been feigning
He'd only been mocking the doctors and nurses
Nurturing resentment, building up a
Thoroughly antagonistic, caustic rage

When they put him back in a few days later
It was clear to everyone in town that this time...
It would be no short stay

But secretly, everyone,
Including the Sheriff and his mother
Breathed a sigh of relief, though they'd never admit it

Securely secluded in his new home
Ben began to scrawl his long, hard to pronounce word
On the sanitarium walls,
With a pen, pencil, or a marker

They curbed this practice at first
By cutting off his access to those items

Ever resourceful,
Ben began to steal things with which to write

Lipstick, ketchup packets, sodas
Anything that would adequately stain a wall
Anything fluid enough to write with
Or could be made so, with water or cafeteria juice
Eventually, he resorted to writing his word
With his feces

After that, they always kept him restrained, tied down
The white jackets with the extra-long sleeves;
That whole deal

Soon after that,
They started the electroshock treatments

It was all unfortunate and heartbreaking
For his poor mother;
The good sheriff did his best to
Console her on Friday evenings

But the oddest part of all of this was how
There was a certain *irony* in it

The electroshock thing that is

I say this because, well,
I seem to (ever so vaguely) recall...
Ben's word did have *something* to do with electricity

Yes! I remember now!
Something about electricity!

I overheard him babbling something
About its application
In the power grids of... *something or other*

To tell you the truth,
I wasn't really paying much attention
But yes, it was something about *electricity!*

Give me just a moment, and maybe I can tell you...
If I can dig it out of my memory
What the word was and what it meant...

Now, let's see... what was that word?

I believe it started with an H...

Or was it an L?

K maybe?

Nope... sorry,

I just don't remember

untitled

on the edge
thin panes of glass

as if these platforms
were not precarious enough
already

we jump up and down
hooting and hollering about
art and ideas

primadonnas
starring into
foggy mirrors
all hot and scratched
by our own breath

whenever our abilities or motives
are called into question,
we produce these
fractured reflections

whipping them out
with a speedy precision
like hardened, seasoned
gunslingers...

look here!

see what *this* says
about *me*!

they look,
but of course

they see only *their* mirrors,
their two-dimensional soapboxes

even when we place the item
right into their hot, little hands

for some odd reason,
the picture is, to them, *blurry*
not as sharp
not so revelatory

a little hazy; lines not quite
as strong as the way that
we see them

the colors, not as bright

and they opt to put their money
back into their wallet
they're saving what they've got
they've got a line on a short runner in the fourth
a sure thing

they're going to bet on a horse, all right;
just not your horse

> *but i'm an artist!*
> *see the beauty of what i do*
> *and who i have become*
> *through doing it!*

and on and on and on
we rant
about visions, form,
sound, and substance
truth

as if we were ever allowed
to get anywhere near
even the front gate
of that elaborate complex
known as truth

when in fact, we can't even
bribe the door guy

we *might* deliver
on that promise
about once
or twice

in a good year

a very
good
year

oh shit

is this your soapbox?

must've grabbed the wrong one

my bad

Ghost Writer

[Dear reader, if you would be so kind as to fill in this page with some clever thoughts, that I might take full credit for them that would be extremely helpful. Your assistance is greatly appreciated]

Part-Time

As I listen to the master, Andres Segovia
who is busy mesmerizing my speakers

I will write, attempt the same greatness

fail
try again

perhaps my great fault is that I have been
too varied in my interests

I have been guilty of being
only part-time

I play chess and poker
I play guitar
I write poetry
I practice kung-fu
I practice magick

perhaps, too many irons in the fire

perhaps, I have been merely lazy;
this seems more likely

I have been a part-time druggie and a drunk;
it has consumed entirely too much of my "free time"

I have sold my forty-hour soul to stupid men
on the pale promises of a stable roof;
all paper-thin, malicious lies

While I'm busy weighing
the pros and cons of movement

sun-dried chess pieces of predicament
there are future incarnations of genius
springing up all around me
strategically placing themselves in
right places, fortuitous times, elbow rub pockets

second coming Coltrane's and budding Bukowskis
I will no doubt buy their albums, eat up their books
Their mastery will no doubt enchant me

I have never been one to
shy away from an open admiration
of mastery in any field,
be it hip-hop or quantum physics

anyone who truly knows me
knows that I become giddy when anyone
steps up to the plate and hits one out of the park

I have been the sole person to
stand up in a crowded theater and clap
when someone gives an outstanding performance
that should've been acknowledged

I am unafraid of the Joneses
unimpressed by their useless, suburban opinions

the likelihood of my own great audience
wanes daily, with the dwindling sun
and every rotting moon

I have yet to pass on any
eternal knowledge

I have perfected
nothing

So, you really liked it?

So,

      you really   liked it?

Did you really
          hear
               the lyrics?

          You know...
             like, really *listen*
                 to them?

Did you
       understand   them?

I'm sorry.

My fault.

     I really should have

          known better

     than to ask.

untitled

all art is
schizophrenia

the only
point of
discussion

is whether
its nature

manifests

as delusions
of paranoia

or delusions
of grandeur

and that point
is moot

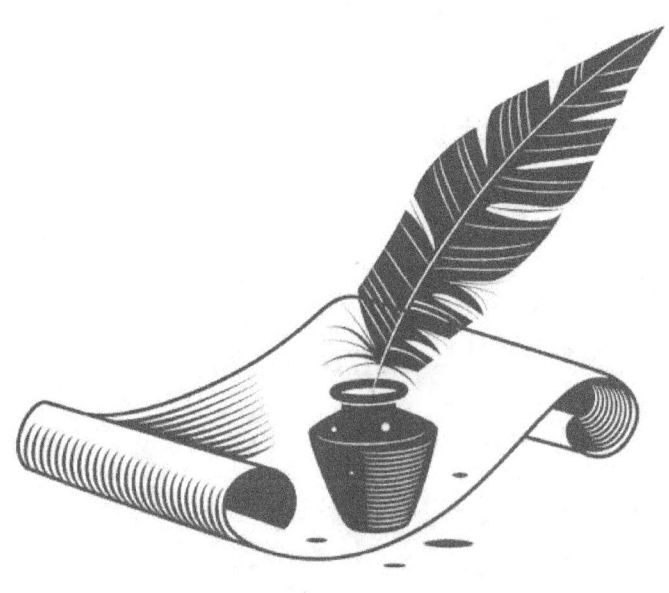

Underwater

I can feel it
Washing over me
Same old thing
As it used to be

And nothing matters
So just smile
Best you can do, baby
Is have some style

Standing in my tears
Drenched to the bone
Don't jive me, baby
But don't leave me alone

And I will write this
Upon the wall
A great struggle now
Brings greatness to all

haiku zero

thousands of millions
none understand poetry
essence of nothing

hindsight

maybe
if i'd never

written
about
you

you
would

still

be here

maybe
you would

not have

become
poetry

ABOUT THE AUTHOR

Kevin Trent Boswell is a thing that briefly blinked in and out of existence. It made noises and gestures while it lasted. The exact nature of its demise is unclear. Some sources say it collapsed beneath the weight of entropy and time. Other tertiary facts suggest the possibility that it was destroyed by a predator, an accident, or perhaps even by itself. The truth of the matter will never be known. Luckily, no one cares.

Examples of its strange behavior:

Chaos Comes Apart

remission

on the page - poems for artists, writers and other hooligans

Liber Ex Liberi - The Book of Children

Next

Dark Matter - Poems of Horror and Depravity

in the current

Out On the Killing Floor - Bleak, dark, dismal, apocalyptic poetry of the most depressing possible variety - The end of all life on Earth & other children's stories

Time for Nothing

patreon.com/magus72

kevintrentboswell.com

www.ingramcontent.com/pod-product-compliance
Lightning Source LLC
Chambersburg PA
CBHW070533220526
45467CB00003B/937